"A rushed journey is a waste of time; you can see nothing. I am here by the grace of God; I must take advantage of it and examine nature carefully, for I shall never return to these waters again. Instinct tells me to let myself drift with the swift current. Reason stops me: For an explorer, hurrying through an unknown land is like running away from the enemy."

"I am sitting on my little bench, my ship's compass in front of me, my notebook on my lap. I am recording our course as we go along."

"The virgin forest—what they call 'tall timber' in Guiana—has a cold, forbidding look to it. Countless colonnades 100 or 120 feet high. From them issue the songs of birds with incomparably rich and variegated plumage."

"This band of Indians, which could have been mistaken for a moving forest, streamed alongside us at an easy trot."

"Uanica climbed up a nearby tree.
He was holding a long, thin pole
to which he had fastened a piece
of rope, forming a noose. He
slipped it around the animal's
neck and gave it a sharp tug."

CONTENTS

THE AMAZON
PAST, PRESENT, AND FUTURE

Alain Gheerbrant

DISCOVERIES

HARRY N. ABRAMS, INC., PUBLISHERS

NEW YORK

12

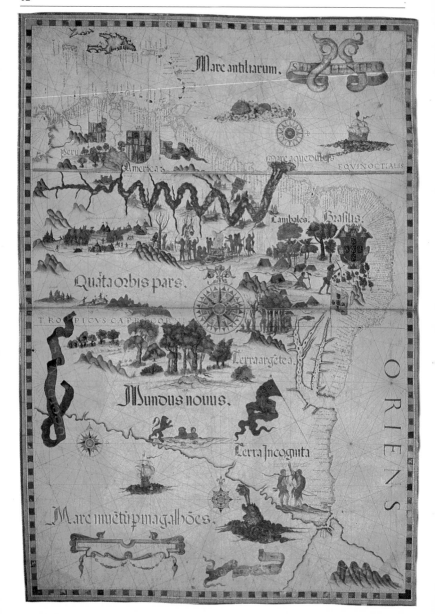

"Why did the Indians defend themselves in this manner? It must be explained that they are the subjects of...the Amazons, and, our coming having been made known to them, they had gone to them for help, and there came as many as ten or twelve of them. We saw the Amazons in front of all the Indian men as women captains, fighting so courageously that the Indians did not dare to turn their backs, and if they did the women clubbed them to death before our very eyes."

Gaspar de Carvajal

CHAPTER I
CINNAMON IN THE AIR

"With eyes wide open, the conquistadors lived in a lucid and endless delirium."
Jean Descola

Although Vicente Yáñez Pinzón (who had commanded the *Niña* on Christopher Columbus' first voyage) first sighted the Amazon delta in 1500, the discovery of the land beyond it, which came to be known as the "Green Hell," did not begin for another forty years. And it came not from the Atlantic, but from the lonely glare of the Andean altiplano, an unforgiving land conducive to migrations, mirages, and dreams.

The conquistador Francisco Pizarro (left).

After a Perilous Journey, Gonzalo Pizarro Reached Quito on 1 December 1540

Two hundred Spaniards, half of them on horseback, accompanied Pizarro as he set out from the Peruvian capital of Cuzco with orders from his older brother, the conquistador Francisco, to take over as *gobernador* of Quito, a thousand miles to the north. Their ranks were bound to thin along the way; so when he found his cousin, the brilliant lieutenant-general Francisco de Orellana, founder of Guayaquil, welcoming him at the city gates and putting himself at his disposal, a heartened Gonzalo was quick to accept his offer.

Orellana knew full well that this administrative shuffle—the naming of a new governor—was, in fact, a pretext for an altogether different mission so ambitious and thrilling that he insisted on joining up. So the two men struck a bargain. Orellana would head back to Guayaquil to muster all available manpower and equipment. Gonzalo would take office in Quito, make preparations for the upcoming campaign, and wait for his cousin to return.

They both hailed from Trujillo in Estremadura, Spain, as did Balboa, Cortés, the other Pizarros, and

many other conquistadors. Seasoned campaigners by the age of thirty, they had weathered many an ordeal since the conquest of Peru had begun, seven years earlier. But neither had any inkling of the strange turn of events that awaited them during their next adventure.

An Imposing Barrier of Perpetual Snow Loomed East of Quito: What Lay Beyond?

Cinnamon—at least that was the rumor. Open country carpeted with cinnamon! In an age when spices were as alluring

Fifty-three of the loftiest volcanic peaks in the Andes rise above the altiplano of Quito on one side and foothills sloping down to the Amazon on the other.

Spices, valued not only for their culinary applications, but for medicinal properties we are only now starting to rediscover, played an unexpectedly pivotal role in the exploration of the world. Cinnamon is an antiseptic, a powerful digestive, and a respiratory stimulant.

as gold, there was magic in the word. Hadn't Columbus himself sought a cinnamon route? Who could tell—this scent just might lead to El Dorado!

It took Pizarro less than three months to prepare. An acting governor of Quito took office on 18 February 1541. With no sign of Orellana, three days later Pizarro decided to leave without him.

The procession that marched out on 21 February onto the Andean altiplano and toward the peaks of the Cordillera made for an unbelievable sight. Leading it were three hundred and fifty armored *hidalgos* (two hundred of them on horseback), followed by two thousand ferocious dogs trained to attack Indians, and four thousand "volunteer" porters (conscripted Indians) laden with weapons, provisions, and, to quote 16th-century chronicler Garcilaso de la Vega, "iron, axes, hatchets, hemp ropes, and nails." Next came two thousand similarly burdened llamas, and two thousand hogs brought up the rear. The Spaniards marched into the Cordillera each carrying nothing more than a sword, a small shield, and a supply kit.

The weather deteriorated; they were pelted by torrential, windswept

Peru was the source of a river of gold that in less than twenty years washed over Europe and had even upset its geopolitical balance. The river began in the Andes, where jewelry, sacred vessels, and sculpture snatched from Inca temples were melted down to ingots in compact Spanish-built furnaces. From there commandeered llamas transported the treasure-turned-commodity down to the coast, where the gold bars were then loaded into galleons.

Crossing the Andes.

rain. Horses slipped on the snow-clad rock, the column slowed, and Indians started collapsing. This first ordeal alone claimed a hundred of them. Then came forests so dense that their only path was the one they themselves hacked out, a foot at a time, with axes and machetes.

Meanwhile, Orellana had set out behind them and was advancing by forced march. Although less encumbered and therefore more mobile, he was harried by bands of Indians. By the time he finally caught up with Pizarro a month later, he had lost all his horses and gear. His twenty-one surviving men carried nothing but their swords. The journey thus far had been so grueling for all concerned that they had come only thirty leagues (approximately ninety miles) from Quito, though Pizarro thought it was sixty.

Pizarro decided to explore ahead with a small party, leaving the main

Gold fever and the allure of spices inspired unreasoning greed in Spanish soldiers and turned these rugged sons of a stinting land into ruthless conquerors.

Indians not already cowed by the Spaniards' horses were utterly terrified of their specially trained dogs. Pizarro brought two thousand ferocious Indian-attacking dogs on his expedition (left).

body of the expedition with Orellana. Seventy days later he finally reached what he hoped would be the Promised Land. And he found cinnamon trees, all right, but they were so few and so scattered they could not be farmed commercially.

So keen was Pizarro's disappointment that he threw half of his guides to the dogs and burned the other half alive. He and his party then headed north, discovered a "fair river," met up with some peaceable Indians, and promptly made off with sixteen of their canoes.

After Orellana and the other men caught up with him, they all labored along the banks of this river for about sixty miles until it emptied into a much larger waterway "half a league wide," according to the expedition's chronicler, Dominican friar Gaspar de Carvajal. At this juncture Pizarro decided to stop long enough to build a brigantine. The boat could just accommodate twenty or so

passengers, and into it were crammed all the heavy equipment and the ailing remnants of the four thousand "volunteers" recruited back in Quito. The name of the village that now stands at this site, near the confluence of the Coca and the Napo rivers in Ecuador, is El Barco—a reminder of their ship.

The expeditioners started out again, most of them trudging along on foot since they had only the sixteen canoes in addition to their little brig. Fresh hardships awaited them: They had to maneuver around marshes and improvise bridges, and provisions were running low. Before long they had slaughtered the last of the pigs. After about two hundred miles, morale flagged.

Since they had been told that in just a few days they would reach prosperous villages, Orellana suggested that he take sixty men and the brigantine and canoes downstream to forage for food. Pizarro acquiesced, and Orellana shoved off. It was 26 December 1541—a day Pizarro would come to rue, for he never saw Orellana or his shipmates again.

Once Pizarro and his men had eaten the last of the dogs and remaining hundred horses, they had to turn back, embittered and enraged at Orellana's

In the 16th century explorers looked upon Amazonian Indians as neither "noble savages" nor ferocious headhunters. Acknowledging their humanity, the conquistadors called attention to those differences that accounted for (though did not excuse) the natives' ignorance of the True Faith. Engravings from the time reflect the Spaniards' attitude.

presumed treachery. It took them six months to struggle back overland to Quito. It took Orellana only slightly longer to discover the mightiest river on earth.

"I Celebrated Mass, as is Customary at Sea, to Commend Our Souls and Lives to God"

Gaspar de Carvajal was among Orellana's contingent and kept a detailed diary of the expedition. "The current was so strong," he notes, "that we covered twenty-five leagues (approximately seventy-five miles) a day from the very start, and it would have been all but impossible to sail back against it." What's more, the prosperous villages they had been promised did not materialize. They were forced to press on.

One long week later the Spaniards finally heard the sound of drums beating in the jungle, and a village came into view. Orellana presented the local chieftain, Aparia, with some purple clothes and promptly pronounced him a subject of Emperor Charles V, in whose name he officially took possession of the chieftain's domain. Orellana christened this the "land of Aparia the Lesser," for he soon learned that downriver there lived another Aparia, a far more important overlord he called Aparia the Great.

The detachment deliberated on the promise they had made to Pizarro. They all agreed that it was virtually impossible to labor back up the 750 miles of raging river they had just negotiated. It would be better to keep going and make their way back to Peru by sea, which, judging by the river's steadily increasing width, they felt could not be far off.

Since canoes would hardly do for an ocean voyage, Orellana concluded that a second brigantine had to be built. Coarse soldiers turned into impromptu woodcutters and charcoal makers; the hardest part was forging the two thousand nails they would need. A month went by, and relations with the Indians began to sour. Orellana decided it

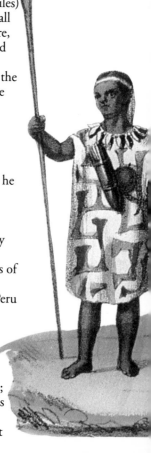

The anonymous 19th-century artist who drew these Indians called them Napo after the river along which they lived. They belong to the Shuar nation—better known as the Jívaro—of Ecuadorian Amazonia.

was time to move on; besides, there would be plenty of time to assemble the boat downriver.

Before setting out again, however, the shrewd leader contrived to get himself unanimously elected captain-general and representative of the Spanish crown in Gonzalo Pizarro's stead. A document to that effect was drawn up, countersigned by the entire contingent, and duly witnessed by a scrivener. Whereupon Orellana offered a thousand castillanos—equal to about nine pounds of gold—to any six men willing to go back and bring the news to Pizarro. Only three volunteered: Given the ordeals they were bound to

The Indian groups Gonzalo Pizarro, Francisco de Orellana, and their men encountered from the Río Coca to the mouth of the Napo were probably all Shuar. They were famous for their practice of shrinking trophy heads.

face, they would not be enough. The idea was dropped. The expedition struck out again.

On 11 February 1542 They Unknowingly Sailed Out of the Napo and into the Amazon Proper

A fortnight of travel brought them to Aparia the Great. Orellana and his men claimed to be the Children of the Sun and, not surprisingly, were given an especially polite welcome by their awestruck hosts. There was plenty of tasty food. This was an ideal spot, the Spaniards determined, for assembling the second brigantine. Caulked with kapok cotton and fish oil, it was launched on 24 April.

On 12 May, as the Spaniards sighted a large, bustling village, they were set upon by a large flotilla of armed canoes with warriors hidden behind tall shields and "threatening us as if they were going to devour us." Although two days of fierce fighting left one Spaniard dead and fifteen wounded, they managed to raid the Indians' stores of food, including several thousand turtle eggs (enough to feed "an expeditionary force of a thousand men for a year," adds Carvajal). The region they were now passing through—Machiparo territory—was unquestionably the most populous they had encountered thus far. Then they reached Omagua land, where for more than a hundred leagues "there was not from village to village a

Pizarro stated his reasons for building the first brigantine in a letter to the king. "It was [because of] food and the problem of transporting weapons and the munitions for the harquebuses and crossbows, and of taking along the sick, and shoes for the horses, and iron bars and pickaxes and shovels and adzes, for already the greater part of the porters…had died."

Contemporary views of a Napo Indian camp (opposite, above), and the Spanish party building a ship (opposite, below) and attacking an Indian village.

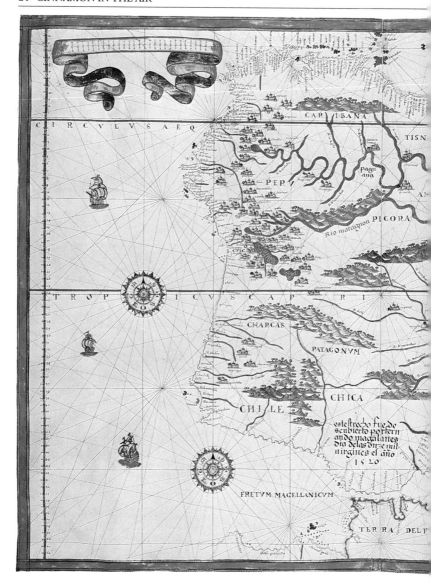

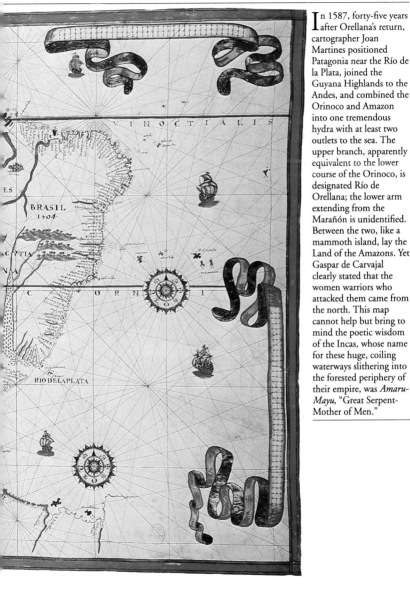

In 1587, forty-five years after Orellana's return, cartographer Joan Martines positioned Patagonia near the Río de la Plata, joined the Guyana Highlands to the Andes, and combined the Orinoco and Amazon into one tremendous hydra with at least two outlets to the sea. The upper branch, apparently equivalent to the lower course of the Orinoco, is designated Río de Orellana; the lower arm extending from the Marañón is unidentified. Between the two, like a mammoth island, lay the Land of the Amazons. Yet Gaspar de Carvajal clearly stated that the women warriors who attacked them came from the north. This map cannot help but bring to mind the poetic wisdom of the Incas, whose name for these huge, coiling waterways slithering into the forested periphery of their empire, was *Amaru-Mayu,* "Great Serpent-Mother of Men."

crossbow shot."

Well into what is now Brazil, the party sailed past the mouth of the Japurá and on into waters that looked as black as ink; consequently, they named this river the Río Negro. Later on the legendary rubber capital of Manaus rose at this site.

The Amazons: Not Just a Legend?

As they went on the Spanish put in at Indian villages, some of them fortified, and took on fresh provisions —usually at swordpoint. On 5 June 1542 they landed at a "medium-sized" village that Carvajal believed to be the land of the Amazons. It is a fanciful episode in his otherwise-realistic account. "In this village," he writes, "there was a very large public square, and in the center was a hewn tree trunk ten feet in girth, there being represented and carved in relief a walled

city with its enclosure and gate. At this gate were two towers, very tall and having windows, and each tower had a door, the two facing each other, and at each door were two columns. Two very fierce lions, which turned their glances backward, held between their forepaws and claws the entire structure, in the middle of which there was a round open space. In the center of this space there was a hole through which they offered and poured out *chicha* for the Sun, for this is the wine which they drink. When asked by the captain what that [signified], an Indian answered that they were subjects…of the Amazons and that the only service they rendered them consisted in supplying them with feathers to line the roofs of their temples, and that the villages they had were of that kind."

Depictions of Amazons from the 16th and 17th centuries. Sacred instruments (center) are still sounded at village entrances to ward off ancestral spirits stalking the Amazonian night.

On 24 June there was a memorable encounter with "Amazons" during a battle "so fierce we all came very close to perishing." "The Amazons go about naked," Carvajal notes, "but with their privy parts covered, with their bows and arrows in their hands, doing as much fighting as ten Indian men." There was another ambush the following day as they drifted close to shore, but the only casualty was Friar Carvajal himself. "Our Lord saw fit that an arrow should be shot in one of my eyes, and in such a way that it went through to the other side, from which wound I have lost the eye and even now am not without suffering or free from pain."

The Spaniards Travel Through a Land of Fantasy and Hostile Indians

The expedition sailed past the mouth of the Xingu. Gradually the rain forest gave way to savanna, and the gladdened soldiers drifted across expanses of rich prairieland just waiting to be turned into wheat fields, vineyards, and cattle pasture. But arrows shot by "tall men with cropped hair and skin dyed black" brought this idyll to an abrupt end. One man died in a few hours from a slight scratch: The Spaniards had just been introduced to curare.

The Arawak of the Orinoco-Negro region sent two-tone signals with slit-log drums.

Now fleets of several hundred canoes, each filled with twenty to forty warriors, tried to block the way as throngs cheered them on from the banks. It must have been quite a spectacle, with the reports of harquebuses punctuating drumrolls, bellowing

"Anyone who has seen them busy with their bows will agree with me that, naked as they are and without any armlet, they can draw and shoot them so fast that, with due respect to the good English bowmen, our savages, holding their supply of arrows in the hand with which they hold the bow, would have fired off a dozen while they would have released six."

Jean de Léry
1575

trumpets, and lilting Indian panpipes. "They came on with a frightening din," Carvajal reports, "but it was a marvelous thing to see their squadrons on the riverbank dancing about and waving palm branches."

The tide was rising at a furious pace, so the Spaniards knew the Amazon estuary could not be far off. The expedition reached Marajó Island in mid-July. Carvajal reckoned that since their departure they had covered a distance of about 4500 miles. So what if his calculations appear to be a bit exaggerated! The important thing was that no one had ever accomplished such a journey down this river that no one, in fact, had ever known existed.

Unaware that the Portuguese settlements of Pará lay just to starboard, the explorers veered to port and into a maze of tiny islands inhabited by fearsome Carib Indians who kept them continually on the run. Then

"The satisfaction I have derived from watching foot soldiers with their golden [helmets] and gleaming weapons cannot compare with the pleasure I took in watching those savages fight."

Gaspar de Carvajal

The coast of Brazil, from a 1602 engraving (below).

the smaller brigantine struck a stump and foundered. So it was back to making charcoal and forging iron, fighting when they weren't busy with repairs.

At long last, on 26 August 1542, the banks of the river parted and the sea came into view. The sailors had no charts, no compass, no sextant. No matter: They headed north and hoped for the best. The ships promptly drifted apart, and each gave the other up for lost. A few days later, much to the Spaniards' surprise, both ships anchored at Cubagua, a small island off the coast of Venezuela.

Would Brazil Be the Site of a "New Andalusia"?

The first journey down the Amazon was history. It had taken eight months to get from the Andes to the Atlantic. (It had taken another ten just to cross the Cordillera to the Coca.) Eleven men perished along the way; fighting had claimed only three of them.

Gonzalo Pizarro, who had marched out of Quito with three hundred and fifty conquistadors, two hundred horses, two thousand dogs, and four thousand Indians, staggered back on foot with eighty fellow Spaniards. Not one Indian, horse, or dog had survived. When he arrived he learned that his brother Francisco had been assassinated in his palace and that he himself had been relieved of his duties by Emperor Charles V. No doubt out of desperation, Gonzalo raised an army and led an open revolt against the viceroy. The age of the conquistadors ended in Cuzco on 11 April 1548, when Pizarro was beheaded.

For his part, Gaspar de Carvajal went back to Lima and was later appointed archbishop. He died peacefully in 1584, at the age of eighty-two.

What became of Francisco de Orellana? His new dream was to return and colonize the lands he had just discovered, as Cortés and Francisco Pizarro had done. Off he rushed to petition the Castilian administration for the royal patent he felt was rightfully his. In 1544 he was appointed governor of the Amazon

Although Charles V (above) happened to be born the very year Brazil was discovered, he hardly went out of his way to perpetuate the concern his predecessors Ferdinand and Isabella showed toward American Indians. No doubt he was too busy implementing his new continental strategy, which, incidentally, he owed to the influx of gold from the New World. Nevertheless, the promulgation of the New Laws (1548), which prohibited Indian enslavement and recognized their status as human beings, forged a lasting link between his reign and the history of the New World. It took centuries, however, for such directives to acquire the force of law.

territory now officially known as the province of New Andalusia. Orellana left Spain with four ships and four hundred men, but in the New World he found that their ranks—and his dreams—crumbled before his very eyes. Twice he tried to assemble a brigantine in the Amazon delta, as he had done before. Twice he failed, as if history refused to repeat itself.

He finally succumbed to fever and died, never again to see the main channel of the river that temporarily bore his name.

This engraving of Gonzalo Pizarro's execution may have been intended as an object lesson in the vagaries of chance, but the artist's staging smacks more of the theater.

The Amazon: The Great Serpent-Mother

The lower course of the Amazon looks like an inlet lazily snaking its way across a vast expanse of flat, open country. From the air the carpet of rain forest looks as unpenetrated now as it did at the dawn of time. Its monotonous basin spans 2170 miles from east to west and over 600 miles from north to south. Its banks are more than 6 miles apart downriver from Manaus—1000 miles in from the coast—and soon widen to about 20, then about 60. Extending more than 200 miles from end to end, the Amazon delta envelops gigantic Marajó and the crowd of smaller islands where Caribs and Orellana fought so fiercely. A hundred miles out to sea westbound ships that have not yet sighted land run into a huge plume of muddy freshwater flecked with floating jungle debris: It is the Amazon, so powerful it travels all that distance before it begins to disperse.

It is hard to tell where reality leaves off and imagination begins in a world that delights in blurring distinctions between life-forms—between animal, vegetable, and mineral; air and water; light and shadow: A leaf can turn into a butterfly, a liana into a snake, a snake into a liana. In the 16th and 17th centuries the brooding rain forests of Amazonia witnessed an adventure-filled epic of men in breathless pursuit of illusion.

CHAPTER II
LIVING
LEGENDS

There are always two sides to myths and symbols—the inspirational and the sinister. Amazonia was no exception, as can be seen in this 16th-century map (left). Right, a somewhat later view of "America."

The Legend of the Amazons Did Not Begin with the Discovery of America

Homer made mention of the Amazons as early as the ninth century B.C. Through the centuries their realm, first thought to lie in the Caucasus and then in the heart of Scythia, shifted west to Cappadocia, Chaldea, Africa, and finally to one of those mysterious islands Marco Polo had heard about. Small wonder that Christopher Columbus expected to discover this island somewhere near the New World, as did Amerigo Vespucci and other great explorers steeped in classical culture.

Indeed, the Isle of the Amazons shifted so far west that one day it emerged from the ocean and ended up deep in the tropical rain forest we now call Amazonia.

But Friar Carvajal's account infused the myth with a freshness and plausibility it had never had before. In 1542, for the first time ever, the fierce women warriors had actually been seen, even engaged in combat. The people who took part in the adventure said so themselves.

Even though the Spanish court

"Conquered and seized by the Greeks," we read in Herodotus, "the Amazons fled to the land of the free-ranging Scythians. 'We would have you for our wives,' they said, to which the women replied, 'Nay.... Your women abide in their wagons working at women's crafts and never go abroad a-hunting or for aught else.'"

did not take Orellana's reports seriously, a symbolic chain reaction rooted deep in our collective unconscious had been triggered in the imaginations of everyone intrigued by the mystery of equatorial America. It swept history along with it and took several centuries to subside.

Various views of the Amazons in relief, tapestry, and engraving.

The Myths of the Amazons and El Dorado Soon Became Inseparable

At the time the Cordillera of the Andes was believed to be the home of an overlord known as El Dorado. According to tradition he would be coated with gold dust and ritually immersed in what has since been identified as Lake Guatavita (near Bogotá) while sacrificial offerings of jewels and vessels were thrown into the water.

The truth of the matter was that his powerful altiplano neighbors, the Chibcha, had dethroned him even before the Spanish arrived on the scene. But what did history matter? Turning their backs on the Andes, the Spaniards sought El Dorado—and the Amazons—far from there, northeast of the Río Negro, at a place on the western edge of the Guiana Highlands where cartographers drew a fabulous lake bigger than the Caspian Sea. In time, once imagination gave way to geographical fact, Lake Parima became Sierra

"We draw the bow, throw the javelin, ride horses: We are not housewives!"

Jacques Lacarrière

Parima, mountainous source of the Orinoco.

The shores of this mythical lake were thought to be the site of a city of stone "that far exceeds any of the world, at least so much of it as is known to the Spanish nation." This was the capital city of Manoa, supposed home of El Dorado, now described as a "great emperor." A man named Juan Martínez had reportedly lived there for seven months.

"He was not allowed to wander into the country anywhere. He was also brought thither all the way blindfolded....After Martínez had lived seven months in Manoa and began to understand the language of the country, Inga [the emperor] asked him whether he desired to return to his own country or would willingly abide with him. But Martínez, not desirous to stay, obtained the favor of Inga to depart, with whom he sent divers Guianians to conduct him to the River Orinoco, all laden with as

El Dorado (below left) was said to live in Manoa, whose scope befitted a legendary city: According to Sir Walter Raleigh, Juan Martínez reportedly walked its streets for more than a day before reaching the emperor's palace.

much gold as they could carry, which he gave to Martínez at his departure. But when he arrived near the river's side, the borderers, which are called Orinocoponi, robbed him and his Guianians of all the treasure…save only two great gourd bottles filled with beads of gold curiously wrought, which those Orinocoponi thought was [his] drink…. So in canoes he fell down by the river of Orinoco to Trinidad, and

So vast it's a wonder no one ever saw it, Lake Parima (here in a 1630 Dutch map) was by far the biggest and most persistent hoax ever perpetrated by geographers. It took two centuries for them to remove it from their maps.

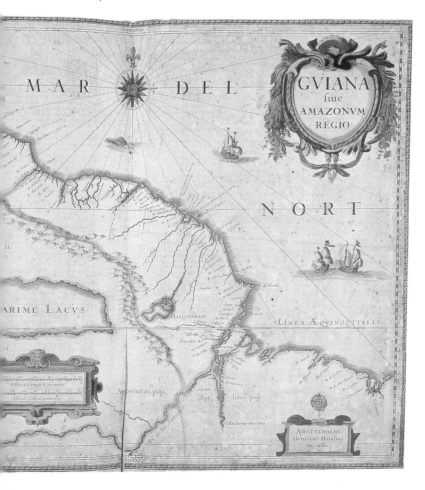

from thence to Puerto Rico.... For the abundance of gold which he saw in the city, the images of gold in their temples, the plates, armors, and shields of gold which they use in their wars, he called the city El Dorado." At any rate, that is what Sir Walter Raleigh, favorite of Queen Elizabeth I, claimed to have read in the papers of the governor of Trinidad, whom he had taken prisoner.

The realm of the Amazons was believed to lie near Manoa. According to Martínez, "these women…wear long dresses of fine wool and golden crowns several inches across. They accompany with men but once in a year. If they conceive and be delivered of a son, they return him to the father, if of a daughter, they nourish it and retain it. All being desirous to increase their own sex and kind, as many as have daughters send unto the begetters a present…a kind of green stone known only to them."

After languishing in the Tower of London for thirteen years Sir Walter Raleigh (above) made a second voyage to the fabulous land of El Dorado in search of the greatest adventure of them all. He then returned to England—and the block.

Sir Walter Raleigh Forsook the Pomp of the English Court and Set Sail in Search of Manoa

Nobleman, occasional poet, privateer if not pirate, Raleigh was a larger-than-life figure who never abandoned his dreams. Raleigh weaves into his account, *The Discovery of the Empire of Guiana*, particulars about the two myths that compelled him to leave everything behind. His description of the land of the Amazons enlarges on and further embellishes Carvajal's: "Their cities, all built of stone, are connected by paved roads, these being lined with walls, which have at their entrance manned gates opened only to those who pay a toll. Round about, herds of vicuña graze in rich pastures."

Like miniatures in an equatorial Book of Hours, Raleigh's tableaux make the future Green Hell out to be an earthly paradise. "I never saw a more beautiful country, nor more likely prospects, hills so raised here and there over the valleys, the river winding into diverse branches, the plains adjoining without bush or stubble, all fair green grass, the ground of hard sand easy to march on, either for horse or foot, the deer crossing in every path, the birds toward the evening singing on every tree with a thousand several tunes, cranes and herons of white, crimson, and carnation perching on the riverside. The air fresh with a gentle easterly wind, and every stone we stooped to take up, promised either gold or

Seen welcoming Indians in the 16th-century engraving below, Raleigh began writing his monumental (and, unfortunately, unfinished) *History of the World* in the Tower of London.

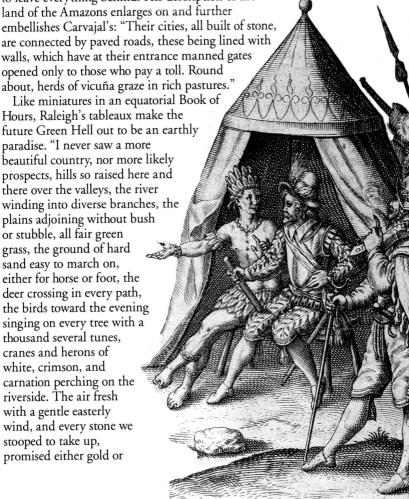

I. la Trinidad. MARE del NORT.

Terra di PARIA.

Orenoque F. *Capuri F.*

silver by its complexion. Your Majesty shall see of many sorts, and I hope some of them cannot be bettered under the sun." The region had so many of these stones, all one had to do was bend down and pick them up. "The Spaniards call it 'The Mother of Gold,'" adds Raleigh without further comment.

Unfortunately, Queen Elizabeth died soon afterward. Raleigh's second voyage ended with an inglorious retreat to the Antilles. For all his fertile imagination, this adventurer and reputed Prince Charming did not prove as fortunate as Scheherazade and, like Gonzalo Pizarro, was beheaded on his return to London in 1618.

The Wonders of the Past Go Hand in Hand with the Exploration of the New World

Christopher Columbus had set the tone in a ship's log that sometimes reads like the adventures of Sinbad. He fully expected to find Cyclopes ("men

The Ewaipanoma (also called Acephali, "headless men") may have been the present-day Yekuana, a Carib people of northern Venezuela.

with a single eye in the middle of the forehead") on the island of Cuba and felt sure that equally strange creatures "with snouts of dogs, who ate men" lay in wait nearby.

But Amazonia, it seemed, sheltered even greater wonders. After describing the Tivitiva, who "dwell upon the trees," Raleigh writes about the Acephali, deformed creatures famous throughout Europe for their monstrous anatomy.

Perhaps these were Pliny's Blemmi, then thought to dwell in Africa. If so, their reappearance was short-lived. Captain Laurence Keymis, who took part in Raleigh's second voyage (1617), made the following entry in his diary: "A cacique [local chieftain] imparted to me particulars relative to the headless men, said to have their mouths in the middle of their breasts. The legend of the Acephali originated from the fact that these people are given to keeping their shoulders in a raised position,

Everything about this land was alien and defied conventional logic. As these 16th-century engravings demonstrate, the first Europeans to set foot in Amazonia let their imaginations run away with them and claimed actually to see and hear everything they had hitherto only imagined: from the works of Pliny to Herodotus, from the words of Arabian storytellers to Mogul writers, from tales of knightly derring-do to medieval hagiographies, from cathedral gargoyles to the all-too-lifelike visions of Hieronymus Bosch. Seldom have reality and fantasy complemented each other so well.

The fanatical missionaries who started hounding the "savages" of Amazonia in the 16th century were largely responsible for the exodus of Indian populations toward the interior. Forced to defend themselves against a systematic assault on customs and beliefs dismissed out of hand as devil worship, the Indians unreluctantly slaughtered their overzealous intruders when they saw fit. The missionaries (including Spanish priest Ferrer in 1611, at left, and another, anonymous, missionary, opposite), in turn, saw the opportunity to earn the crown of martyrdom as further incentive and redoubled their efforts. This absurd conflict did not begin to subside until Christendom acknowledged the right of every individual to be different.

as they consider this deformity graceful."

By then, the tug-of-war between history and legend, fact and fiction, was already well under way. In 1575 André Thevet, a Frenchman who had spent three months in Brazil, retracted what he had said about the Amazons in *Les Singularités de la France antarctique* (*Peculiarities of Equatorial France*): "They are not Amazons, only unfortunate women who endeavor to preserve their lives, children, and property while their husbands are away."

In 1560 Lope de Aguirre, an Obscure Subordinate Officer, Proclaimed Himself King of Amazonia

Was there anything to the stories about El Dorado, Lake Parima, and the fabulous city of Manoa? To answer this question, in 1560, less than twenty years after Orellana's expedition, the viceroy of Peru instructed a Spanish general, Pedro de Ursúa, to journey across the Cordillera and find out for himself.

No sooner had Ursúa's hastily raised band of men reached the Amazon than a Basque named Lope de Aguirre mutinied, executed his general, and proclaimed himself not only commander of the detachment but king of Amazonia. And anyone unwilling to follow him would be thrown to the crocodiles!

As Aguirre headed north in search of the Guiana Highlands, did he unknowingly discover the Casiquiare, a natural waterway linking the Orinoco and the Negro rivers, more than a century before Humboldt did? Be that as it may, he emerged at the mouth of the Orinoco, across from Trinidad; and after seizing Margarita, the island of the pearl fishers, he was defeated by royalist troops from Venezuela and, needless to say, sentenced to death.

Before he was beheaded, he reportedly uttered the following brief prayer, probably the only one ever to pass his lips: "Lord, if you intend to do me a good turn, do so right away. Save your glory for your saints." A fitting epilogue to his story.

Gonzalo Pizarro, Lope de Aguirre, Sir Walter Raleigh—heroes or cutthroats, they all lost their heads over Amazonia in more ways than one. Aside from rapacity, the only thing these men had in common was their craving for the super-human and the wondrous.

At the end of his long odyssey, Lope de Aguirre ruled supreme over Margarita Island for two months after killing the governor and leading officials. Bent on carving out a bigger empire for himself in Venezuela, he then decided to head back to the mainland, where, forsaken by his cohorts (and, the story goes, weary of being a professional cutthroat), he fell into the hands of Spanish royalists and was executed.

Missionaries in the Amazonian Rain Forest

Fresh attempts were made to penetrate Amazonia early in the 17th century. Even before reaching the

main river channel, several missionaries lost their lives at the hands of the same Indians who had clashed so fiercely with Gonzalo Pizarro.

Still, the missionaries' time had come. Following in the footsteps of the conquistadors, Jesuit priests and Dominican friars established numerous, if temporary, missions and in so doing became the first to compile valuable ethnographic and linguistic information. On one occasion, Jesuit priest Cristobal de Acuña reports, a canoe with two missionaries and six Spanish soldiers drifted downstream to Pará, near the mouth of the Amazon, "and all they could tell us was that they had come from Peru, seen many Indians, and dared not go back the way they had come."

A Portuguese Captain, Pedro de Teixeira, Was the First to Journey From Pará to Quito—and Back

One day, nearly a century after Orellana's discovery jolted the world—especially the rival courts of the Iberian peninsula—the governor of Pará, who resided in the new city of Belém, finally decided to organize an expedition. He instructed a veteran, Captain Teixeira, to journey up to Quito and record

The armadillo, as described by Sir Walter Raleigh: "A beast called by the Spaniards *Armadilla*...seemeth to be barred over with small plates somewhat like to a *Renocero*, with a white horne growing in its hinder parts, as big as a great hunting horne, which they use to winde instead of a trumpet. Monardus [a physician] writeth that a little of the powder of that horn put into the eare, cureth deafnes."

———

Sixteenth-century explorer Jean de Léry accurately describes the agouti as "a reddish-brown creature the size of a month-old pig, which has cloven hooves, a very short tail, ears much like those of a hare, and very good to eat."

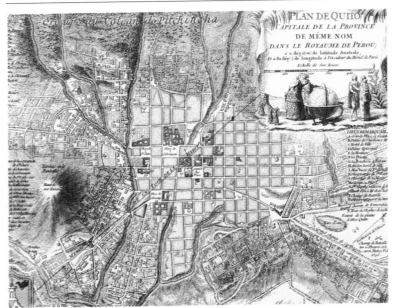

everything he deemed noteworthy along the way.

Teixeira crossed the Pará border on 28 October 1637 with a flotilla of forty-six canoes laden with sixty Portuguese soldiers, twelve hundred Indians, and sundry wives and guides—some two thousand souls in all. Before it was over, more than half of them were to run away.

Even so, the first journey up the Amazon was completed in the record time of eight months. On 24 June 1638 Teixeira reached the first Spanish settlement, near Quito.

The Amazons, According to a Dominican Friar and a Jesuit Priest

The astute viceroy of Peru gave the Portuguese a polite welcome and promptly directed that Teixeira be provided with whatever equipment he would need for the trip back, including, as Father Acuña notes, the assistance of "two individuals in whom the crown of

What conqueror did not eventually turn into a builder of cities? The Spanish were no exception. No sooner had Pizarro seized the Inca empire than he started planning its facelift. Atahualpa was put to death in 1533; his dynasty expired with him. In 1534 Sebastián de Benalcázar, Pizarro's lieutenant, razed the capital city and mapped out a new Quito with a Spanish-style grid of streets. Set like a jewel amid mountain peaks, this priceless vestige of Jesuit architecture 9500 feet above sea level has been remarkably well preserved.

Castile can place its trust regarding everything that has been discovered thus far and which is likely to be during this return voyage."

The *corregidor* of Quito himself personally volunteered for the mission; instead, Crown officials chose Acuña, who had recently arrived from Spain to found a Jesuit college.

Thus, a hundred years separate the first two accounts of the discovery of the River of the Amazons—one by a Dominican, the other by a Jesuit. In December 1639 Acuña reached Belém and immediately set sail for Spain, as he had been instructed to do. His book, *The New Discovery of the Great Amazon River*, was published in 1641. Comparisons between Acuña's and Carvajal's narratives are as interesting as they are inevitable.

Before proceeding to the journey itself, Acuña pointedly states that some accounts "may not always be as truthful as they ought to be"—a passing gibe at Carvajal. "But this one will be, and indeed I shall allege nothing I myself cannot attest to with my head held high, and more than fifty Spaniards, Castilians, and Portuguese who made the same trip will vouch for those things declared as certain or dubious, as the case may be."

Yet, from the very first chapter, he makes a case for the Amazons, arguing that he heard about them wherever he went and that "the details, on which there is universal agreement, are so precise, it is impossible that a fiction should have entered into so many languages and be met with among so many natives."

Certain details of Father Acuña's description of the Amazons bear repeating, if only to show his

The classicism of these *all'antica* figures smacks more of a drawing by Michelangelo than the sketchbook of an explorer in the New World. These illustrations from Jean de Léry's account of his voyage to Brazil (1555-8) depict scenes from the life of the famous man-eating Tupinambá.

tendency to wax lyrical. "As a rule, these worthy women have no commerce with men. Even when those [men] with whom they do have intercourse make their annual visit, they do not welcome them without weapons in hand—bows and arrows—and so remain until such time as they have judged the men and are satisfied that they have indeed come in peace; whereupon they lay down their arms and run to their guests' canoes. Each of them takes hold of a suitable hammock—which is what the men sleep in—and carries it back to her hut and hangs it up heaven knows where."

His conclusion, however, is equivocal. "Time will reveal the truth about this, and whether these are indeed the famous Amazons, and if their land holds treasures which might enrich the whole world."

"It was wonderful to hear the women, who yelled so loudly it sounded like the howling of dogs and wolves. 'He is dead!' some of them wailed, 'he who was so brave and gave us so many prisoners to eat.' Whereupon the others replied, 'What a good hunter and excellent fisherman he was!' Then one of them cried out, 'Oh, our avenger, our gallant slaughterer of Portuguese!'"

Jean de Léry

We need look no further than this classicizing, indeed courtly, tableau of prettified Indians by a contemporary of Jean-Jacques Rousseau to see that the age of the "noble savage" had arrived. Paradoxically, even as rapid strides were being made in objective documentation of the new continent, the way its inhabitants were being portrayed was never farther from the truth.

Particulars About Indian Life and Customs in Acuña's Account

Certain aspects of Acuña's narrative signal the approach of the Enlightenment, and from them we can gauge the progress that had been made in the century between his account and Carvajal's. He documented not only animal and plant species indigenous to the Amazon and its banks, but plants the Indians cultivated, the tools they used, their customs, their hunting and fishing techniques. Even if these notations fall short of bona fide scientific observations, at least they point to an emerging shift away from fantasy.

Acuña points out that the Amazon's four principal resources are wood, cocoa (which in those days grew wild along the riverbank), tobacco, and sugarcane, followed by cotton, sarsaparilla, gums, resins, and pharmaceutical oils. Add mineral deposits, and you have a complete rundown of what was to become—and still is—the backbone of Amazonia's economy.

Yet, a few pages later, this conscientious observer reports the existence of giants "ten to sixteen spans" (over ten feet) tall; of dwarfs "no bigger than tender babies," known as the Guyazi; and of "people with their feet turned backward, so that pursuers track them in the wrong direction."

By the End of the 17th Century Amazonia Had Been Incorporated into the Brazilian Empire

Acuña concludes that the banks of the Amazon, "paragon of rivers," are "paradises of fertility, and if art abetted the richness of the soil, there would be nothing but peaceful gardens along its entire length." Acuña's discourse reeks of the courtier. "Though it holds magnificent riches, it is open to all. Indeed, it

An American native, the tobacco plant.

magnanimously bids people from every walk of life to profit therefrom: to the poor, it offers sustenance; to the laborer, his fill of work; to the tradesman, business; to the soldier, the road to glory; to the rich, newfound wealth; to the powerful, lands to govern; and to the king himself, a whole new empire."

This undisguised invitation notwithstanding, Spain did not attempt to wrest Amazonia from Portugal: The two million square miles that comprise the bulk of the basin were to remain a permanent part of Brazil. But this vast plain was to be ringed by a Castilian Amazonia bordered by present-day Venezuela, Colombia, Ecuador, Peru, and Bolivia.

By the end of the 17th century the partition of Amazonia was complete; Spain and Portugal had been the only real contenders. English, French, and Dutch navigators found their claims shunted to the north, to the other side of the Guiana Highlands.

For all intents and purposes, the establishment of a fort at Belém on 20 January 1616 signaled the beginning of Portugal's annexation of Amazonia. Once the other Europeans withdrew and Captain Teixeira completed his journey to Quito, the next stage of Portuguese penetration was the fort at Barra (1669)—the future Manaus. Magistrates along the river soon outnumbered even soldiers.

"With an enthusiasm that bridged every barrier, they climbed the Andes, they swept down dark mysterious rivers, they trekked across the deserts, and struggled through the Laocoön entanglements of its firefly-spangled jungles.... America [was] investigated, codified, and put into a literature that freed the continent completely from the fantasies which had flourished for three hundred years."

Victor Wolfgang von Hagen
South America Called Them

CHAPTER III
THE AGE OF REASON PENETRATES THE RAIN FOREST

Fauna, flora, and crafts of Amazonia from 19th-century lithographs.

Just as exactly one century (1540 to 1640) separated the first two books about the exploration of the Amazon, a hundred years elapsed between Acuña's chronicle and what could be called the first scientific account of a journey down the Amazon.

La Condamine: Amazonia's Window on Modern Times

In 1745 the French Academy of Sciences in Paris heard Charles Marie de La Condamine read his *Abridged Narrative of Travels Through the Interior of South America, From the Shores of the Pacific Ocean to the Coasts of Brazil and Guiana, Descending the River of the Amazons.*

The stated purpose of La Condamine's expedition was to settle a purely scientific controversy: Did the earth bulge at the equator and flatten out at the poles, as Newton maintained, or vice versa? A team of botanists, astronomers, and the most distinguished savants of the 18th century set out with La Condamine on a journey to Quito to calculate the exact length of a degree of longitude when measured at the equator. Once his official mission had been accomplished, La Condamine decided to stay and embark on a journey down the Amazon.

His account does not so much separate fact from fiction as cross-fade them (to borrow a term from cinematography), blurring myth at the same time as bringing objective description into sharper focus.

INTRODUCTIC
HISTORIQUE:
ou
JOURNAL DES TRAVA
DES ACADEMICIEN
Envoyés par ordre du Roi sous l'E'qu

Depuis 1735 jusqu'en 1745.

Tous ceux qui ont pris quelque part à la que la Figure de la Terre, ont remarqué avec surprise ans ont à peine suffi pour terminer notre voyage. On estimé la durée à quatre tout au plus : encore suppe alors, conformément au premier projet, qu'outre la du méridien, à laquelle nos opérations se sont bornée rapporterions cette de quelques degrés de l'équateur ; de travail dont les ordres du Roi nous ont depuis dispi

D'ailleurs on fait que le voyage au cercle polair le plan ne fut formé qu'après notre départ, & que l d'un degré, dans les régions incultes & souvent dé

A

Charles Marie de La Condamine (left) on curare: "It will no doubt occasion surprise that among a people who possess an instrument so certain and so quick of effect, with which to satiate their vengeance, jealousy, or hate, it should be fatal to monkeys or birds alone. It is the more to be admired that a missionary, ever dreaded and often held in abhorrence by his neophytes,…should live without fear or mistrust of harm."

> "Though no remaining vestige should be found of this feminine republic, this would not yet prove that none such had ever existed.… If ever such a nation [of Amazons] did exist, it must have been in America, where the frequent wanderings of the women, who often accompany their husbands to war, and the hardships of their domestic life, might originate [the] idea of shaking off the yoke of their tyrants."
>
> La Condamine

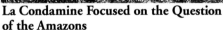

La Condamine Focused on the Question of the Amazons

First, he noted a consistency of detail in the folklores of peoples otherwise so mutually alien as to rule out any suspicion of complicity. Everything, he wrote, led him to believe that after migrating from south to north, the women warriors settled in the heart of Guiana. Later, in 1800, Alexander von Humboldt assumed "not that there are Amazons,

Gorges along the Amazon, 1745 engraving.

…but that women in different parts of America, wearied of the state of slavery in which they were held by men, united themselves together, like the fugitive Negroes."

That fastidious intellectuals like La Condamine and Humboldt did not debunk the myth directly may come as a surprise. Since stories about the Amazons were so widespread and persistent, they probably did not feel they had enough hard evidence to settle the issue of "feminine republics in the New World." We should point out, however, that at about this time a few informed observers with firsthand knowledge of the Indian world seemed more than willing to deflate the legend. The captain of the frigate *Solano*, dispatched by the king of Spain to oversee the first official demarcation of Portuguese Brazil from Spanish Venezuela, mentions in 1756 that Guipuinavi women, particularly newlyweds, fought alongside their husbands and displayed exceptional bravery—understandably so, he adds, as they were hot-tempered and were taught, like boys, how to handle a bow and shield from early childhood. "These women or others like them," he concludes, "must be the Amazons Orellana saw fighting among the men, because, then as now, women from here [the upper Orinoco] to the Amazon joined in the fighting."

Accurate Information About Mountains and Rivers Was Gradually Incorporated into Maps

Without Amazons, the imagination was losing ground in Amazonia. The women warriors were the first to go. Then Lake Parima, the fabulous city of

"Alexander von Humboldt [left] has been with me for some hours this morning. What an extraordinary man he is! Though I have known him so long, I am always newly amazed by him. He possesses a versatility of genius which I have never seen equaled. Whatever may be the subject broached, he seems quite at home with it, and showers upon us treasures in profusion from his stores of knowledge. He is like a fountain with many spouts: One need only proffer vessels to collect its precious and inexhaustible flow."
Goethe

Humboldt crossing the Cordillera (right), from a 19th-century engraving.

Manoa, and the palace of El Dorado disappeared from the map. Commissions with geometers and surveyors started to demarcate boundaries across what was still largely unexplored terrain.

One long-standing error, attributable in large part to the El Dorado legend, involved the location of the Guiana Highlands. Another perpetuated the difficulty in distinguishing between the Orinoco and Amazon river systems.

In the late 18th century people finally realized that the river Colombians upstream called the Putumayo and Brazilians downstream called the Içá were, in fact, the same major tributary flowing down from the Andean Cordillera into the Amazon, and that likewise the Japurá and Caquetá were simply Brazilian and Colombian names, respectively, for the same waterway. Neither of these two rivers flowed directly into the Orinoco or the Negro, as had long been thought. Farther north, the Meta, Vichada, and Guaviare, which run more or less parallel to

La Condamine had already raised the question of possible links between the Amazon and Orinoco basins. To settle it, Humboldt journeyed up the Orinoco in 1800, traveling, as locals did, in *falcas*, large, half-decked canoes with palm-branch roofs. Motorized versions of the same kind of craft ply the Negro and upper Orinoco to this day.

the Içá and the Japurá, turned out to be branches of the Orinoco.

The Casiquiare River, the connection between the Negro and Orinoco rivers.

Humboldt Credited with Discovering the Link Between the Orinoco and the Amazon

The question was not whether a link between these two mighty rivers existed—there were too many accounts of it to doubt that—but how they were connected and where. After all, if there was no link, how could Indian flotillas encountered in one river turn up in the other? How could Lope de Aguirre have left the Amazon and reached the sea by way of the Orinoco delta? In 1742 a woman claiming to be from Venezuela had made her way to Brazil by way of what she said was a river flowing from the Orinoco to the Río Negro. Two years later some Jesuits reported that a missionary from the Negro sailed upstream to call on the superior of the Orinoco missions; the two of them sailed back down together by the same route.

The earliest authoritative maps of the region were

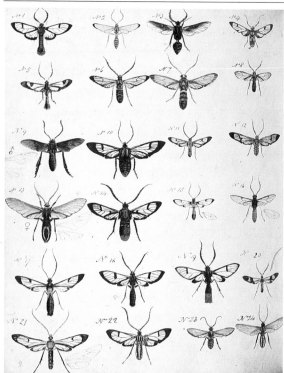

The Industrial Revolution of mid-19th-century England left in its wake a new breed of scientific researcher, one that did not depend on privilege to make good. Consider Henry Walter Bates and Alfred Russel Wallace, still remembered for their contributions to natural science. When they first met and found they shared a dream of adventure, one was a surveyor's assistant, the other a hosier's apprentice. The British Museum commissioned them to compile a collection of insects and plants—at threepence for every specimen received "in salable condition"—and in 1848 they landed at Belém with nothing to declare but their enthusiasm.

A fish Wallace discovered during his travels on the Negro.

riddled with inaccuracies. Sanson based his on the observations of Father Acuña. The second map (1707), which reflected forty-five years of fieldwork by Father Samuel Fritz, a German Jesuit, was already closer to the mark. It took another hundred years to see the light. But in this land of disproportion, where so much water flows simultaneously in so many different directions, how could the matter have been puzzled out any sooner?

Alexander von Humboldt's achievement was to describe in black and white the course of the

Casiquiare River, which he himself had negotiated in 1800 from its confluence with the Negro to its starting point on the upper Orinoco. Once and for all, the Andes and Guiana Highlands were correctly assigned their respective waterways.

That the Casiquiare truly existed and was navigable was truly momentous news, coming as it did on the eve of an Industrial Revolution that was to change the face of the world and expand trade between the continents on either side of the Atlantic.

River dwellers began to move away in droves. La Condamine was the first to call attention to the irreversible exodus the arrival of soldiers and missionaries had precipitated. "More than a century back," he writes, "the banks…were peopled with a great variety of nations, who withdrew to the interior at the sight of the Europeans."

"These Devoted, Hard-Working Men Plying the Amazon Have Come, Not to Ravage, But to Study"

That was how botanist, zoologist, and early ethnographer Alcide d'Orbigny characterized the scientist-scholars of the 19th century. The era of great scientific explorers did, in fact, coincide with a relative lull in the slaughtering of Indians. Although the

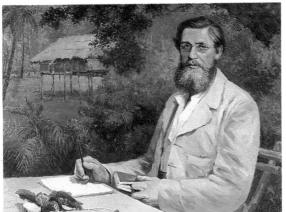

Henry Walter Bates spent eleven years in Amazonia and brought back 14,712 specimens, including eight thousand species unknown to science. He became a luminary in the field of entomology and advanced the theory of mimicry, which helped pave the way for the discovery of the evolution of species. Two of his drawings are above and at left.

Alfred Russel Wallace, the father of zoogeography, spent four years on the Río Negro. A precursor of the theory of evolution, he sent Darwin his paper on natural selection, which was read to the Linnaean Society in London at the same time as the first draft of the renowned *Origin of Species*.

majority of them were naturalists—
botanists for the most part—they were
all "philosophers" in the tradition of the
Enlightenment and, like Humboldt,
generalists. (In those happy times
specialization did not preclude working
in several fields at once.) They
spontaneously pioneered Amazonian
ethnography. Their accounts are our
window on the lives of what were at the
time still undisturbed Indian groups.
The fact that most of these peoples are
now totally acculturated, when they
have survived at all, makes the work all
the more intriguing.

Long, frequent journeys were now the
rule as many Europeans crossed the
ocean. Botanist Auguste de Saint-Hilaire
trekked across thousands of miles of
Brazilian jungle to compile an herbarium. D'Orbigny
ranged across the continent and returned to Paris
with a collection of 100,000 specimens so valuable
that his findings form the basis of numerous studies
to this day. There was also the team of Johann Baptist
von Spix and Karl Friedrich Philipp von Martius—
and so many others from so many other countries.

The popularity these scientists enjoyed was fueled
by the enthusiasm of a century that clamored for
fresh discoveries. Public opinion in Europe spurred
them to action and helped release the funds they
needed for their undertakings. The magazine *Le Tour
du Monde* thought nothing of publishing Paul
Marcoy's account of his fourteen-year odyssey from
the deserts of coastal Peru to Belém—for three years
running! Not since the chronicles of the Spanish
Conquest had so much been added to our understanding of the continent. The mounds of notes,
collections, and specimens they brought back with
them have been an inexhaustible resource for
scientists and historians ever since.

"They wrap a rope
around its neck, suspend
it from a tree, and
clamber up the snake like
a mast until they reach
the neck, then slit its
throat with a knife and
ease themselves down to
the ground, cutting it
open along the entire
length of its body."

Malte-Brun

A Giant Water Lily Big Enough For a Coiled Boa to Nap On

The countless discoveries made in Amazonia at this time range from the amusing to the deadly serious, from the picturesque to the momentous. In the 1840s, while exploring what was then British Guiana, botanist Robert Schomburgk stumbled across a spectacular water lily of gigantic proportions. Stretching about six feet across, the pad looked like an enormous pie plate and could have easily supported a coiled boa napping in the shade of its tremendous blossom, which boasted an expansive corolla that ran the gamut of pink between its pearly white petals and bright red center. Here was a flower worthy of Amazonian excess. The chivalrous Schomburgk christened the future pride of botanical gardens *Victoria regia* in honor of the British sovereign. But there were even more valuable, if less benign, discoveries to come, discoveries that once again turned the River of the Amazons into the stuff that myths are made of.

Charles Bates catching a crocodile, one of the two most spectacular monsters of Amazonian waters. The black caiman can reach sixteen to twenty feet in length; its cousin along the Caribbean coast, *Crocodylus intermedius*, can reportedly exceed twenty-five feet. Some people claim that anacondas (opposite) can grow to about forty feet and weigh more than three hundred pounds.

Río Branco Indian

Uerequena Indian

Conibos Indian

Mayorunas Indian

Uaupé Indian

Macuxy Indian

Philosophical Journey

Between 1783 and 1792 a group of Portuguese explorer-scholars gained prominence by compiling the century's most valuable collection of illustrations devoted to Amazonian Indians and fauna. Alexandre Rodrigues Ferreira was a doctor of "natural philosophy" at the University of Coimbra; his traveling companions, Joaquim José Codina and José Joaquim Freire, were artists from the Royal Natural History Collection in Lisbon. They painted continuously for nine years while ranging about 24,800 miles (a distance equivalent to the circumference of the earth) along the Negro, Branco, Madeira, Guaporé, and Mamoré rivers. Surprises awaited them at every turn; they were the first, if not to see, at least to record them with photographic precision. One such discovery, a device used to propel arrows or javelins, is one of humanity's oldest weapons, predating even the bow (opposite, lower left).

Hummingbird

Trogon

Porcupine

Black
Spider
Monkey

Howler Monkey

Peccary

Collared Anteater

Woolly Spider Monkey

The Science of Illustration

Testimony to their unerring powers of observation, Codina's and Freire's illustrations for the *Diario da Viagem Fillosofica* (*Journal of a Philosophical Voyage*) lavish as much detail on indigenous Amazonian wildlife as they do on Indian weaponry and adornment. Known to Brazilians as the *beija-flor*, or "kiss-flower," the tiny, brightly colored hummingbird looks like a masterpiece of precious enamelwork. The peccary, a local food staple because of its tasty, nourishing meat, lives in herds of up to a hundred individuals. The Indians hunt them with spears, but are careful not to squander nature's bounty and take only what they intend to eat or cure for the rainy season, which is their winter. The spider monkey is the only one in the world that swings from branch to branch using its arms and prehensile tail. The name of the bulkier, more sedentary howler monkey is misleading, for the sound it makes in the forest at sunrise and nightfall is closer to a moan than a howl.

Cotinga

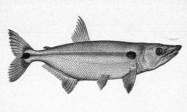

Piranha

Snowy Egret

Cock-of-the-Rock

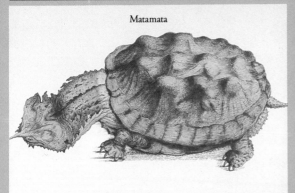

Matamata

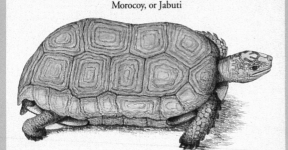

Morocoy, or Jabuti

Crocodile

The Misadventures of a Manuscript

The reputation of the piranha (or cannibal-fish, from *caribe*, its name along the Orinoco) is well established. We should point out, however, that it is not tiny, as was once thought, but as big as a carp. The cock-of-the-rock is coveted by collectors of American birds everywhere for its elegant saffron plumage and fan-shaped crest. Lastly, the matamata, a bizarre turtle that looks as though its head got caught in a funnel, has a distinctive nonretractile neck and must swing its head in under its carapace sideways. Ferreira's monumental collection reached Lisbon unscathed, only to face fresh perils. Geoffroy Saint-Hilaire made off with it during the Napoleonic Conquest, and Ferreira died in 1815 resigned to the permanent loss of his life's work. The manuscripts were recovered but subsequently dispersed and not recompiled for another century.

"A tree called *heve* grows in the province of Esmeraldas. With a single incision it secretes a milky-white fluid that gradually hardens and darkens on contact with air.... The Mayan Indians call the resin obtained therefrom *cauchu*, which is pronounced *cahouchou* and means 'tree-that-weeps.'"

Charles Marie de La Condamine

CHAPTER IV
THE GREAT RUBBER ADVENTURE

In the 19th century the rain forest was invaded by rubber-hungry businessmen.

This point was of particular interest to the learned assembly that convened at the French Academy of Sciences in Paris to hear La Condamine read his *Abridged Narrative*.

"From the Omaguas the Portuguese of Pará learned the method of forming syringes of the same matter, and pumps which need no sucker. These syringes are made in the shape of a pear, with a neck at the extremity, that, as well as the body, being hollow. Into this neck a cane is fitted.... This, when full being suddenly pressed, the contained fluid is expelled with the same effect as from a syringe. Among the Omaguas it is a very common utensil. When they assemble on occasion of an entertainment, the master of the house never fails to present one of these bottles to each of his guests, and its contents are voided constantly previous to the beginning of a grand dinner."

Thus, one of the greatest conquests in the history of modern industrial technology can be traced back to Amazonian syringes and nozzles. Brazilians recall it every time they refer to a stand of wild rubber trees as a *seringue*, or a rubber tapper as a *seringueiro*.

La Condamine's remarks about the Omagua call for further comment. They filled their syringes with a narcotic substance that could be inhaled or administered as an enema, and the use of drugs accounts for their sharing of the device at gatherings. The first rubber object made in Europe, the pencil eraser, was invented by English chemist Joseph Priestley. He christened it "India-rubber."

Indians Had Been Making Expert Use of Rubber from Time Immemorial

The ball the Maya of Mesoamerica played with was made of rubber, as it was wherever this game is known to have existed (the Taino of Haiti, the Apinayé of central Brazil). The Indians along the upper Orinoco coated drumsticks with rubber. Damp wood caught fire more easily when some of the gum was added to it, and it proved handy for caulking leaks in canoes. As far back as the early 18th century the Indians showed the Portuguese of Pará how latex could be molded into boots and containers, or used as a waterproof coating for canvas.

Macintosh, Hancock, Goodyear, Michelin, Dunlop—Names That Have Become Symbols

Although the growing popularity of bicycles and automobiles was largely responsible for the tremendous surge in world demand that began in 1850 and triggered the great Amazonian rubber rush, credit must also go to a handful of inventors and their now-legendary discoveries. In 1823 a Scotsman named Charles Macintosh won instant fame for manufacturing rubber-coated fabric. Seven years later Thomas Hancock perfected a process to make raw rubber pliable. In 1839 Charles Goodyear discovered vulcanization, which paved the way for the production of the first pneumatic tire.

From then on the history of rubber and the automobile went hand in hand. In 1888 while tinkering with his ten-year-old son's tricycle, an Irish veterinarian named John Boyd Dunlop invented the first pneumatic rubber tire, which he eventually patented. Four years later Edouard Michelin made the first detachable pneumatic rubber tire.

The boom was on. Demand for rubber skyrocketed. With a monopoly on wild rubber trees and the freedom to set its own prices, Amazonia became a vast equatorial Klondike. The precious commodity flowed down the Marañón, Ucayali, Javari, Madeira, Napo, Putumayo, Caquetá, and Negro rivers from Bolivia, Peru, Ecuador, and Colombia, converging on Manaus. As the closest deepwater port offering year-round access to ocean-going ships, the city emerged as the rubber capital of the world. With its unique floating docks loaded with rubber, soon Manaus was awash in gold and poised for an era of unbridled luxury. Were the stories that spurred the Conquest about to come true after all?

G rowing demand for rubber prompted Brazil to internationalize the Amazon in 1867, but the days of Michelins, Dunlops, and Goodyears were still years off. Another decade elapsed before the first freighter dropped anchor at Manaus. After that, however, there was no stopping them.

Mythical Manoa Gives Way to the Living Legend of Manaus

In the early 19th century what is now Manaus was Barra, a garrison village that grew from a small fort the Portuguese had built in 1669 to monitor Spanish movement in the area. When botanist d'Orbigny stopped at Barra in 1830, he noted that its three thousand or so tattered inhabitants traded in everything the region had to offer: dried fish, sarsaparilla, Brazil nuts, turtle-egg oil.

The development of a technique to cure latex changed everything.

Harvesting Wild Rubber

A *seringueiro*, or tapper, made the rounds of his marked trees by following a trail that defined his reserved harvesting zone. To turn a profit, every day he had to "milk" his hundred trees (opposite) within the first four hours in the morning, before the sun thickened the sap and sealed off the wound. Another round of the trees to collect the latex (total daily yield: around twelve pounds), and then it was back to his shack to cure the harvest, smoking it over a smoldering fire of green, acid-rich palm nuts. The liquid latex coagulated on a twirled paddle (left), eventually building up to a seventy- or eighty-pound *pele*, or ball of rubber. This chore behind him, he went back into the forest to gather palm nuts for the next day's curing. Only then did he take time out to eat and steal a little rest.

A Vicious Circle

When the rainy season made tapping impracticable, the *seringueiro* floated his harvest downriver to Manaus, where his *aviador* would be waiting for him (opposite). Once the *peles* were split, graded (above), and weighed (below), this middleman signed a new contract with his client—but only after deducting his earnings from his running tab of trade goods. The *aviador*'s warehouses were crammed with canned foods, beverages, clothing, and everything a wretched tapper could develop a craving for during his lonely months in the rain forest: Small wonder that a *seringueiro* invariably left owing his *aviador* more than when he came. Year after year the tapper who fancied himself "free" simply added yet another link to the chain of debt bondage between himself and his pitiless master.

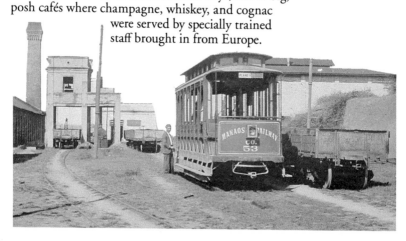

Manaus was built up under Dr. Ribeiro, who became state governor in 1893. "I found a village and turned it into a modern city," he reportedly once declared. When the first electric trolleys (below) began running, three theatrical companies were performing at the newly opened Opera House (left). The city also boasted three hospitals, including one for the insane and one for Portuguese. Home to ten high schools, more than twenty-five primary schools, and a public library, it professed propriety and fostered science.

Rubber was now an exportable commodity. In 1850 Barra was made a provincial capital, renamed Manaus, and allocated its first government funds. That year, it shipped nearly one thousand tons of rubber to Pará. The figure jumped to three thousand by 1870, twelve thousand by 1880, and twenty thousand by the turn of the century.

Manaus burgeoned into a metropolis of fifty thousand. Tatters gave way to attire purchased, if not actually laundered, in London and Paris. Business was transacted, not in *milreis* notes, but in gold coins, and not on the ramshackle tables of olden days, but in big, posh cafés where champagne, whiskey, and cognac were served by specially trained staff brought in from Europe.

Freighters chugged toward New York and Liverpool laden with rubber; they returned full of bankers and pretty women. In short, life on the Amazon was no longer dull.

When the city began to sprawl over marshland, Portuguese paving stones (and the pavers to lay them) were shipped in from Lisbon. Electric trolleys clattered along its ten miles of avenues at a time when Bostonians had to make do with horsecars. Every morning telephone subscribers—there were three hundred when the first lines were installed in 1897— called major stock exchanges the world over to fix the price of rubber. High above the roofs of the city rose the green, yellow, and blue dome of the Opera

"In Amazonia there is a universal love of trade," Alfred Russel Wallace wrote in 1889. "We find the province [of Pará] overrun with traders, the greater part of whom deserve no better name than peddlers, only they carry their goods in a canoe instead of upon their backs." Fifty years later freighters crammed with such goods emptied their holds into huge warehouses, and businessmen prospered.

House, a lavish embodiment of Manaus' golden age.

Created expressly for transatlantic service, the Booth Line inaugurated regular steamship runs between Manaus and Liverpool that same year. The city had truly arrived.

Boom to Bust

Between 1908 and 1910, when Manaus was at the zenith of its power, eighty million rubber trees spread over some 1.2 million square miles of forest were under development. Manaus was exporting eighty thousand tons of raw rubber annually; export duties alone were covering 40% of Brazil's national debt. But the days of the boom were soon over. Seeds smuggled out of Amazonia thirty years earlier had grown into the vast rubber plantations of Malaysia, which would outstrip all competition in terms of yield and production costs. Moreover, trees exhausted by years of relentless tapping were producing a little less latex each year. Amazonia was now on a collision course with financial upheaval.

People started declaring bankruptcy. By 1912 they were selling off their assets at a loss. Empires built as if by magic collapsed like houses of cards. The Opera House closed its doors; nightclubs and luxury shops were shuttered. The only places doing steady business were auction houses, where onetime tycoons divested themselves of jewelry, furniture, and artwork. Notices at Booth Line ticket windows announced that all sailings bound for Europe were booked months in advance. One thing, however, did not change: the timeless indifference of the poor, confined to outlying districts where fat women lazed on thatched-palm verandas while knots of children scampered about barefoot, kicking up dust that turned them red wherever roads gave way to spreading fingers of asphalt and the dark green edge of the jungle beyond.

Yet, that very year, the two-hundred-mile Madeira-Mamoré railroad was inaugurated some twelve hundred miles away. Its purpose was to create an

In the late 19th century the port of Manaus (above) offered all the luxuries a visitor could require—including first-class passage on the Amazon.

"Mad Maria"—that was what engineers nicknamed the colossal, genocidal Madeira-Mamoré Railroad project. Europeans calculated the cost of the railroads they built in their African colonies in human lives per tie. By that standard, this was the costliest railroad of them all. Construction began in 1908 in a particularly remote, densely forested, and disease-ridden area of Brazil and Bolivia. Everything had to be brought in from all over the world by ship, mules, and porters: charcoal from Wales, steel from Pittsburgh, and, ironically, wood from Australia because only termite-resistant eucalyptus wood would do for the ties. The railroad was supposed to have opened the huge rubber reserves of Acre and Madre de Diós to the outside world. But by the time it was finished, five years later, the rubber market had collapsed. Six thousand laborers had perished for nothing.

easier transport route from Bolivia to Pôrto Velho, Brazil, which could be reached by freighters on the Amazon. Slicing through the rain forest, this railway cost an enormous amount of money, took five years to build, and claimed six thousand lives. It was to prove useless: Bolivian rubber was too expensive.

Suárez of Bolivia: The Rockefeller of Rubber

A truly self-made man, Suárez had started out barefoot and become the richest rubber baron in Amazonia. His assets included about thirty thousand square miles in Bolivia, two townships (Riberalta and Villa Bella) on the Beni River, a whole relay system of Suárez and Brothers mooring stations for his own fleet of boats, and exclusive shipping rights on the Madeira. Originally there were seven Suárez brothers, but one of them was killed when he led a company police force into Caripuna territory. Three hundred Caripuna Indians were slaughtered—for one Suárez —and that was that.

The Suárezes claimed these Indians were not good workers: They were lazy, like all the rest, and they were hard to recruit. A friend of theirs on the Madre de Diós River hit upon a novel solution. He rounded up six

The man sporting this stylish moustache would not have looked out of place at a European spa. Rubber baron Suárez emanated the unobtrusive respectability of the truly rich. When his wife died, he built a monument to her in the heart of the rain forest, at Cachoeira Esperanza, above the magnificent falls of the same Madeira River that had witnessed the start of his fortune.

hundred Indian slave girls for breeding purposes and placed his harem at the disposal of his guests. Then all he had to do was wait for their offspring to grow up and get big enough to work.

Arana: A Gentleman of Dubious Respectability

Far less boorish than Suárez, Julio Arana impressed the ladies as being a civilized man, olive complexion notwithstanding. People would talk about his library, his house in London, his children's real English nanny, his predilection for family life. But not much else. Arana was an unobtrusive man, a foil for his nightclub-hopping brothers. Every morning at the same time, he would stride into the offices of the Peruvian Amazon Company—his lifework—and stay cooped up there the whole day.

A shrewd, far-sighted strategist, he knew that Bolivian rubber, the cornerstone of his wealth, was too far away from the marketplace. That is why he backed the proposed Madeira-Mamoré railway.

With busy boat traffic, exports of Amazonian rubber quickly skyrocketed, and consumer prices rose at breakneck speed. In 1900 a chicken at Manaus cost the equivalent of $27, and a bunch of carrots, $9—but the rich got richer and colonial life burgeoned.

"RED RUBBER" ONCE MORE:

On 20 July 1912 *The Illustrated London News* ran a two-page spread on "The Putumayo Revelations"; the headline read "30,000 Lives: 4,000 Tons." The photographs revealed conditions in Julio Arana's Indian camps and showed how, for example, the overseers in the La Chorrera and El Encanto camps beat the Indians' legs with tapir-hide whips that left disfiguring pads of scar tissue.

That is also why he started grabbing 11.5 thousand square miles of forest further north, along the Putumayo: The area was rich in wild rubber trees, deep in a disputed area between Colombia and Peru, and much closer to Manaus. This was also the homeland of the Bora, the Andoke, the Huitoto, the Ocaina—peaceable Indian tribes known since the days of the conquistadors—some fifty thousand souls in all.

Arana recruited a private militia of black men from Barbados, subjects of Her Britannic Majesty. And he had the clever idea of setting up headquarters in London and arranging for City financiers to

THE PUTUMAYO REVELATIONS.

From El Encanto ("Enchantment") camp to *Arbeit Macht Frei*—the motto above the gates of Auschwitz and Buchenwald—the same torturer's humor is exhibited. In this respect, Julio Arana was ahead of his time.

underwrite his firm. That gave it an air of respectability. The sacrosanct militiamen were armed with Winchesters and sent into the jungle to recruit Indians. They rounded up thirty thousand and confined them to company-owned villages.

The Disgrace of the Peruvian Amazon Company

Soon, however, rumors started circulating in London. The treatment of native workers, it seemed, left something to be desired. The City's good name was called into question; public opinion was roused. Five years later a court of inquiry issued a report revealing that the rain forest had been turned into a killing field. All but eight thousand of the fifty thousand Indians in the region had been killed. Each ton of rubber had cost seven human lives.

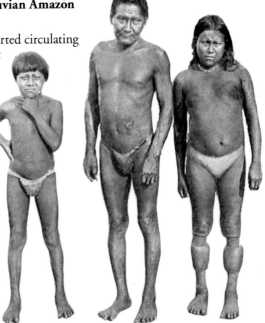

"It is my wish that nothing My Lord the King, my daughter the Princess, and my son the Prince may do, or allow to be done, shall bring any harm to the Indians living either on islands or . *terra firma*, to either their persons or property. Indeed, they shall see to it that these peoples are treated in a just and kindly fashion.**"**

Last Will of Queen Isabella of Spain

CHAPTER V
THE INDIAN AND THE RAIN FOREST

Native people (Puri Indians, left) and animals (an 1820 lithograph of an iguana, right) lived as one with the rain forest.

It is hard to be objective about an inscrutable world whose inhabitants have an outlook so different from our own. The problem between the Indians and us is one of culture. We have given priority to a culture that evolves by working against nature. We think in terms of coercion and conflict: Nature must be subdued. As we see it, having takes precedence over being.

Indian culture, unlike ours, is a process of accommodation to nature. Animals are people like us, the Indians say; trees and mountains have one or more spirits. Indians scrounge, pilfer, and kill, too, if need be—none of which goes against the laws of nature—but they never hoard. Ecology, ever-present, is woven seamlessly into the fabric of their lives.

The Quiet Partnership of Indian and Nature

An Indian's superbly carved and balanced canoe skims the river surface without a ripple. As he trots along his network of practically invisible forest trails, he is careful not to make the slightest sound lest he startle the enemy. Then, whether stalking other Indians or herds of peccaries—killing only what he needs—he suddenly barks as loudly as the packs of hounds that live among certain tribes. In a twinkling, everything falls silent again.

It is common for Indians to hunt with the bow, and they have an endless variety of interchangeable, "customized" arrowheads from which to choose. Lance-shaped points of bamboo, hardened in fire to produce razor-sharp edges, tip arrows designed for use in battle. (The Yanomami also use them to cut their hair.) Feathers are such an important part of body adornment that Indians use special blunted tips, like those on fencing foils, to stun birds and leave the

prized plumage undamaged. But their most sophisticated weapon remains the blowgun, fashioned from a smoothed and polished hollow cane. A single puff can shoot a dart the size of a big needle into a target more than sixty feet away. Although an inch deep, the wound would be slight were the tip not coated with curare, that subtle poison that kills quietly by gradually paralyzing smooth muscle tissue. Bows and arrows are often six feet long, spears ten feet, and blowguns nearly twenty-five. Perhaps the most surprising thing of all is that the Indians are so adept at handling such long weapons in the heart of the densest jungle growth.

"The warlike relations of the whites with most Indian tribes have contributed greatly to the multiplicity of references to weapons from the earliest chroniclers to our own day. In many cases weapons are the only aspects of native culture known to us. Travelers have always shown a particular interest in weapons."
Alfred Métraux

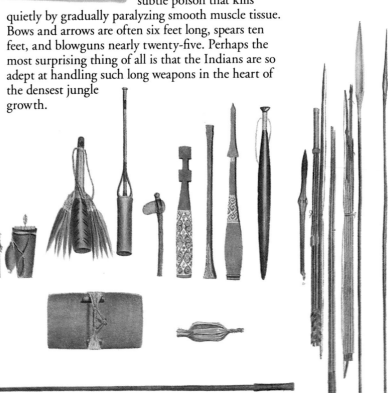

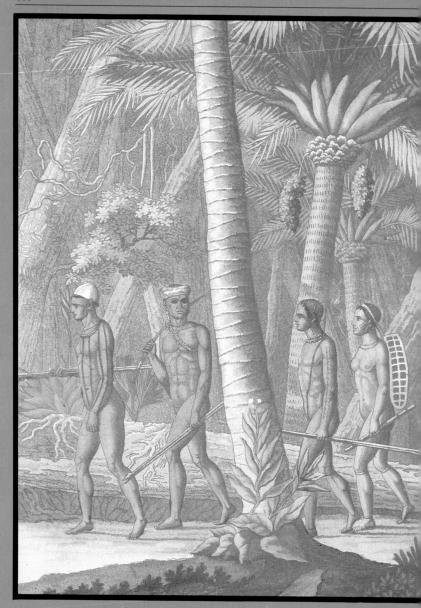

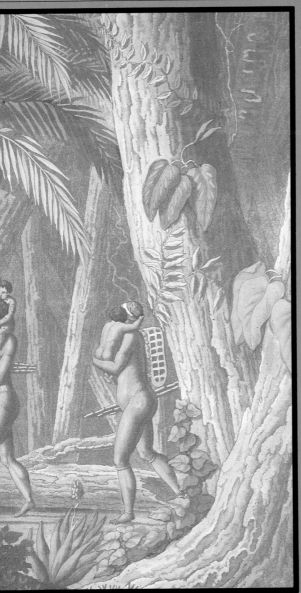

Learning How to Walk

The Botocudo Indians at left demonstrate a point ethnologist Pierre Clastres learned when he asked his hosts, the Aché, to escort him through the forest. They balked. "Their greatest fear was that I might slow them down. Finally, they agreed to go with me, and I quickly realized that their misgivings were well-founded." He was expected to "make a beeline and not waste time. They walked at a brisk clip, and I'd find myself bringing up the rear, impeded if not immobilized by lianas I kept tripping over or by others that would suddenly lash me to a tree trunk. I'd snag my clothes on thorns and make frantic efforts to shake them loose. Not only was I lagging behind, but making a commotion! The Aché, however, were silent, supple, efficient. Before long, it dawned on me that one of the things holding me back was my clothing. Branches and lianas glanced harmlessly off bare Indian skin. I decided to do as they did and shed my clothes."

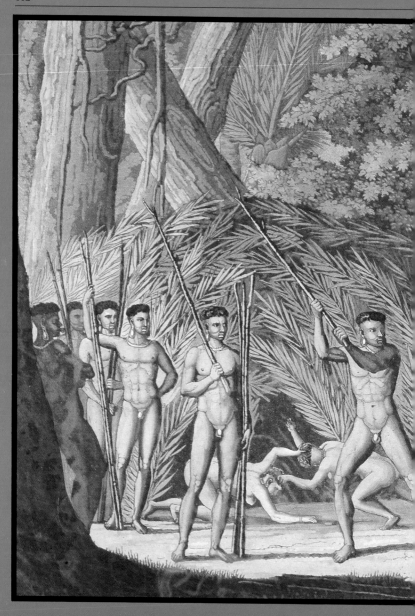

Bacteriological Warfare

Two major tributaries of the Amazon, the Juruá and the Purús, flow through the Brazilian state of Acre, which borders Peru and Bolivia. Since they are navigable along their entire lengths, upriver journeys to their headwaters date back to the early 19th century. The Indians who once inhabited this region welcomed explorers peaceably. Everything changed with the rubber boom, because the area proved to be exceptionally rich in wild-rubber trees. Suárez began building his empire—on the misfortune of Indians. To weed them out as expeditiously as possible, *seringueiros* (prospectors) resorted to techniques the English and French had successfully tried out on North American Indians in the 18th century: They would even hand out disease-infected clothing. Today virtually nothing remains of these peoples.

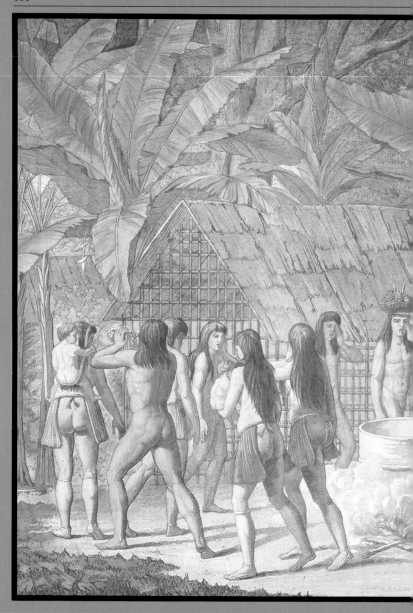

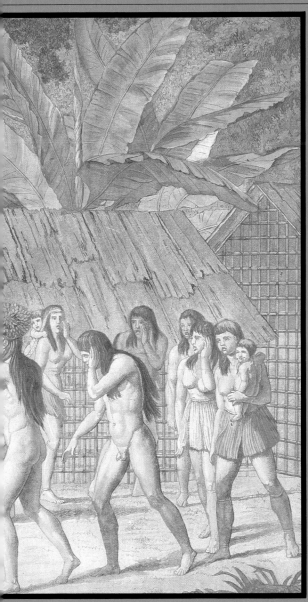

Dancing

Like people the world over, Indians (at left, Camacan Indians) consider dancing both language and celebration, a throwback to a time when there was no clear dividing line between the sacred and the profane. Older than speech (witness the mating dances of birds), dancing transcends speech, for it conveys what words cannot. Now stately, now frenzied, dancing expresses the life instinct whenever it sweeps aside dualities—body and soul, visible and unseen—and makes existence whole again, in an ecstasy beyond time. Certainly countless, often ceremonious, occasionally freewheeling, Indian dances punctuate all of life's events, from the momentous to the pedestrian: birth, puberty, death, war, marriage, building a house, starting a garden.

An Amazonian Invention: The Barbecue

During the dry season, when rivers are at their lowest, the Indians build dams of braided reeds; farther upstream they crush bundles of herbs in the water. The drugged fish rise to the surface and drift down with the current to the dam, where the Indians scoop them up by the basketful. This is known as "*barbasco* fishing," from the name of the plant they use. The next stage was the invention of long, raised softwood racks for roasting and smoking the catch over hot coals. The cured fish would then be ready for storage during the rainy season, when game is scarce. Peccaries and tapirs taken during hunts would be butchered and dressed in the same fashion.

The Indians of Haiti called this rack a *barbacoa*, and the Spanish borrowed the term from them. Thus, the modern barbecue is a good deal more American than people suspect.

A Magical World, the Supernatural Omnipresent

"The Amazonian Indian is apt to sense the presence of supernatural beings in any natural sight that strikes him as strange or awe-inspiring," Alfred Métraux

B arbecuing a tapir (below).

A t a time when the Indian community is besieged by the outside world in ways that threaten its very existence, the continuing presence of the shaman is the surest guarantee of group cohesiveness and, therefore, survival— something both ethnologists and missionaries have had to acknowledge. Diviner, priest, and healer rolled into one, a shaman watches over the health of individuals and is consulted in all matters involving the welfare of his people.

writes. "Waterfalls, certain eddies in the river, oddly shaped rocks are the dwelling-places of cantankerous spirits that bear close watching and must be appeased."

But one cannot ferret out the supernatural unless one knows how to cross over from the visible to the invisible world. Enter the shaman, guide of souls, who can take leave of his body and go off in search of spirits that have been driven away by illness. He also assists his entire people with the difficult life transitions of birth, death, and puberty, for which certain nations prescribe dangerous initiation rites involving copious drink-offerings, tobacco, and hallucinogenic or psychedelic drugs. The shaman's expertise in narcotics, acquired during a very long and perilous apprenticeship, enables him to guide the community toward collective ecstasy and ensure that rituals allowing a safe return to the here and now are properly observed. Some drugs are smoked, others ingested as decoctions, inhaled as snuff, even taken as

Hallucinations and trances are not the prerogatives of shamans. Shared by all, drugs are an adjunct to social gatherings. For example, it is customary for members of the Ouitoto and Yanomami tribes to blow narcotic snuff into one another's nostrils. At such times, drugs not only become a form of property exchange in accordance with the tribe's moral code, but help to liberate the group and promote its psychic well-being in the face of all the evil forces besieging it. This is where psychedelic drugs come in, complementing hallucinogens: Contact with the supernatural need not be a fearful, deadly serious affair.

enemas. Yanomami hunters use *ebene* snuff on a daily basis to sharpen their senses. Elsewhere, the *yopo* found among the Piaroa and most peoples in the region is as famous as their curare and, like it, exchanged during gift-giving ceremonies.

Birds and Feathers: Colorful, Rich Adornment

Playful, imaginative, appearance-conscious, Indians enjoy showing off in front of their peers. Even more than women, men carefully adorn their bodies with skillful designs in red paint from annatto seeds, with occasional highlights in carbon black and blue vegetable dye. Facial designs are in black, red, and white, sometimes given a glossy finish; more intricate and delicate patterns are the rule for women. This gaudy attire is enhanced by many kinds of finery: ear ornaments tipped with long tufts of toucan feathers, large tooth necklaces (proof of a hunter's ability), seed chains, braided-hair ligatures to make arm and leg muscles bulge, lip disks, pectorals, pendants. Palm skirts and feathered crowns or diadems are saved for

"The nakedness of the inhabitants seemed to be protected by the grassy velvetness of the outside walls and the fringe of palm trees: when the natives slipped out of their huts, it was as if they were divesting themselves of giant ostrich-feather wraps. Their bodies, the jewels in these downy caskets, were delicately modeled, and the flesh tones were heightened by the brilliance of their make-up and paint, which in turn seemed to be intended as a background to set off even more splendid ornaments: the rich, bright glint of the teeth and fangs of wild animals among feathers and flowers. It was as if an entire civilization were conspiring in a single, passionate affection for the shapes, substances, and colors of life...."

Claude Lévi-Strauss
Tristes Tropiques

ritual celebrations. On these occasions, the men form solemn processions and display a sharpened bludgeon now used solely for ceremonial purposes, but which Tupi and Carib Indians, among others, once used to execute prisoners during cannibalistic rituals.

The Opening of a Communal House Occasions Festivities, with Several Days of Ritual Intoxication

The communal house is a fundamental symbol. Spacious enough to accommodate a hundred people, it serves as a kind of village square, usually roofed, with living quarters fanning out from the center. It embodies the basic unit of Indian society, which is not the couple, much less the individual, but the kinship group. Depending on age, everyone in a communal house is someone else's child or parent, although couples and their offspring are acknowledged and respected as such. However, several extended families can live together under the same roof. The communal house is also a symbolic representation of their cosmos and cosmogony. It is the one "book" everyone must learn to read.

The tract of cleared land between the village and the surrounding forest is planted with manioc—a source of bread and wine—banana trees, and occasionally a few stalks of sugarcane, pineapple, or papaya. A few years later, once the rains have damaged the roof of the house and washed away the shallow layer of topsoil, the fields are left fallow, and the group moves on to another location, clears the land once again, and

A Curuchu Indian communal house, as depicted in an 18th-century Portuguese drawing (below).

The Tukuna of the Río Solimões (left), a sizable Indian nation at the crossroads of Brazil, Colombia, and Peru, managed to stay on good terms with their white neighbors for two centuries without compromising their sociocultural integrity. However, according to recent reports in the international press, they have become the victims of murderous assaults in Brazil.

builds another communal house. A fresh round of celebration then gets under way.

The Yanomami Can Be Found Slipping Through the Densest Jungles

The Yanomami Indians, whose territory straddles the border of Venezuela and Brazil, probably represent the earliest surviving stage of Indian culture. Perpetually on the move, they lived until recently in complete and unrivaled symbiosis with nature. A Yanomami man would carry nothing but a bow, three arrows longer than he is tall, and a bludgeon fashioned from half a bow. He would keep a few spare arrowheads and a pencil-sized stick with an agouti-tooth tip in a small bamboo quiver that hung down his back.

The Yanomami, basically warriors, live by hunting and gathering and by limited cultivation of native fruit trees. (They scrounge, pilfer, raid beehives, and even catch armadillos in their burrows.) Their diet is rudimentary and, except for meat, their food is usually eaten raw. They sleep curled up in small hammocks made of bark strips. Their rich culture and their lives are

Various types of shelters used by Indians in the Brazilian Amazon.

"Ocelot Spirit, come down into me! *Hekura*, you did not help me. For whole nights I pondered my vengeance. I saw the Vulture Spirit and the Moon Spirit. Moon Spirit was struck by Suhirina's arrow when he invaded the dwelling, eager for human flesh; and from his wound, from his spilled blood, were born a multitude of flesh-eating vultures. Moon Spirit, Vulture Spirit, you are cannibals. Vulture, your head is polluted with blood, your nostrils teem with worms. The dragonflies gather in the sky. Omawe pierced the earth with his bow; out of the hole he made spring a gusher of water that reached the sky and formed a canopy. Up there the dragonflies multiply; up there live the thirsty ones! Let them come down into me! Omawe has burned my tongue! Let them moisten my tongue and refresh it! Those who have ordered the demons to capture our children will receive my vengeance, wherever they may be."

Yanomami shaman's curse on the death of a child, as recorded by Jacques Lizot

intertwined with the overwhelmingly lush—and
haunted—world around them.

The Largest Tribe of Unacculturated People in South America Is Struggling to Survive

Could there be a connection between what was only
recently a very large number of Yanomami and the
fact that they managed to avoid all contact with white
people until modern times? It would seem that way,
teetering as they are now between well-being and
endangerment. At any rate, we know for certain that
the Yanomami people were still flourishing until only
a very few years ago. But they weren't living in total
isolation. In Venezuela, the Yanomami material
culture was evolving—but without borrowing from
the "white world." Over the past quarter century,
they have been adopting certain advances—canoes,
woven cotton hammocks, small banana and manioc
groves—probably as a result of interaction with the
Yekuana, a tribe of sedentary farmers. The two
peoples, weary of feuding, have been exchanging more
than traditions: They are even intermarrying. This
transformation might have proceeded smoothly had it

A third the size of California, Yanomami territory was until recently the last undisturbed sanctuary in Amazonia. The earliest peaceful contacts with Yanomami groups date from the Orinoco-Amazon expedition of 1949-50 (in which the author participated). Back then they were considered fearsome, legendary beings; the Yanomami, for their part, looked upon whites as dangerous, man-eating spirits. Scientific scrutiny of the Yanomami began in the 1960s.

Chances are that the Yanomami would have gone on living in another world, as they always had, if Brazilian prospectors hadn't stumbled upon mammoth gold and diamond deposits on the Amazon slope of Sierra Parima. Thus, El Dorado was reborn at the very spot where the famous adventurer and inmate of the Tower of London, Sir Walter Raleigh, thought he would find it four hundred years ago. Starting in 1987, this gold rush brought forty thousand people—and their culture and diseases —into Yanomami lands.

not been for the intrusion of white people looking for gold and diamonds.

Once Again, Amazonia is Being Overrun by Treasure Seekers

The latest gold rush, which began in 1987, brought prospectors, *garimpeiros*—a pickax in one hand and a Winchester in the other—into the jungle to seek their fortunes. An estimated forty thousand people flooded Yanomami territory in Brazil alone, with estimates of the jackpot reaching $1 billion a year.

Curiously, history repeated itself in the Space Age as hordes of hungry, penniless fortune-seekers trudged toward Sierra Parima to scale a hitherto undisturbed mountain in search of gold. In May 1988 the London-based tribal defense movement Survival International sounded the alarm: "Today the Yanomami Indians are facing the most serious threat to their survival ever. Twenty thousand miners have overrun their territory in the last month alone."

The implications of such an influx of people have been vast. The delicate balance between people and nature has been upset, and the Yanomami are paying the price. Diseases brought by miners—malaria, tuberculosis, venereal disease—have killed at least fifteen hundred Brazilian Yanomami. In 1990 *Time* magazine quoted one Yanomami man as saying,

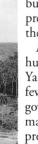

"They gave us rice and wheat, but then we got sick. They pretended to be our friends, but they are killing us."

As word of the crisis spread, a huge outcry in support of the Yanomami built, and within a few years the Brazilian government was engaged in a massive effort to eject the prospectors from Yanomami lands and to set the land aside for the Yanomami alone. In April 1991 Brazilian president Fernando Collor de Mello issued a number of decrees reserving a huge swath of land for the Indians and prohibiting others from entering. On the other hand, though, the reserve has been divided into many sections separated by zones in which the *garimpeiros* and other treasure seekers circulate freely, disturbing the Yanomami. What's more, the parceling of their territory has undermined the Yanomamis' ability to hunt and gather successfully.

But even if the Yanomami and other Indian tribes survive the threats to their health and to their culture, the impact of the white invasion is indelible. Change is inevitable; the Yanomami will never be the same. "The question is," says Venezuelan anthropologist Roberto Lizaraldi, "whether it will be on their terms or someone else's."

Covering an area in eastern Amazonia equal to England and France combined, the iron mine and associated development projects collectively known as Grande Carajas are aimed at catapulting Brazil to world power status.

Backed up by the very latest in technology, the latter-day invaders are broadening their field of operations over the whole of the Amazon basin, from its very heart to its outermost reaches. Prospecting for minerals—not to mention unprecedented quantities of precious stones and metals—has turned up fresh deposits of iron, coal, oil, bauxite, uranium, copper, and lead, inviting development by big business.

Every Day More of the Rain Forest Goes up in Smoke

Like its inhabitants, the rain forest itself is threatened from all sides by mining activity, by intensive

A string of mighty dams provides hydroelectric power for both Grande Carajas and a massive agricultural program. Some thirteen thousand Indians used to call this region home. For them progress translates into an all-too-familiar aftermath: epidemics and pollution introduced by whites, deforestation of traditional hunting grounds, and social disintegration.

cultivation of nutrient-poor soils sucked dry by modern farmers large and small, by logging.

However, it is not so much big business (when managed efficiently) that is responsible for the appalling deforestation currently underway throughout the whole Amazon basin as it is traditional farmers. Slash-and-burn farming, of little danger when sporadic and confined to very small patches of forest (the Indian practice), hastens widespread soil degradation and erosion.

Pollution Has Taken its Toll on the Pirarucu, the Giant Fish of Amazonia

Development has affected the flow of water in the Amazon basin, which not only serves as an irreplaceable transportation network but provides indigenous communities with fish to supplement the animal protein otherwise limited to what they get by hunting in the forest. Over much of the Amazon proper, the growing number of gigantic dams and rapidly escalating pollution of major rivers have

Large-scale industry is not the only source of water pollution. Gold miners use mercury to recover the precious metal and foul the river with its poisonous residue.

already all but wiped out the huge, but harmless, pirarucu, once a staple of the region because it routinely weighs four hundred pounds. In the early 20th century trade in dried or salted pirarucu was still such that it was commonly referred to as the freshwater cod.

Upriver, in mountain streams, the mercury gold miners use has killed off fish along hundreds of miles of river; in some regions game is scarce and the soil so poor that manioc roots do not weigh a fourth of what they do elsewhere. Thus, yet another scourge— malnutrition—is taking a toll on village populations.

A number of dams have been built indiscriminately, flooding preserves once inhabited by thousands of surviving Indians for the sake of producing, some say, negligible amounts of energy.

Indians: A Raw Material Ruthlessly Exploited by Tour Operators

Traditional ways of life are threatened by development. The huge pirarucu, once an Amazonian staple, is now found in only limited numbers.

In some cases the Indians themselves—especially if they sport feathers on their heads—become a developable resource and fall prey to tour operators who prod them into degrading "reenactments" of their own lives. This undermines the distinct identity of these peoples whose perfectly balanced relationship with their environment has led more than a few admiring observers to conclude that, occasional cannibalism aside, it is they who are the civilized ones and we, the savages.

A living legend as a peacemaker and staunch defender of Indians, Colonel Rondon began his military career at the age of sixteen as an army private. In 1910 he founded the Indian Protection Service in the name of the positivist ideal emblazoned on the Brazilian flag. It was the first government agency of its kind in the Western Hemisphere.

Utopian dreaming, some will say. Very well, then, let us speak realistically: Over the years a highly placed Brazilian official has unabashedly stated that, humanism or no, Indians would never stand in the way of development. The current population of Brazil stands at 153.8 million, but some experts predict that the figure will rise to 200, then 300, and eventually 500 million. In light of such forecasts, 200 thousand Indians in the forest do not seem to count for very much.

Indians Discussing Indians

The threat has not gone unheeded, and a new trend is emerging as the century draws to a close. Some Indian peoples (most Indians in the temperate areas of the Andean Cordillera, long accustomed to living near whites, and several large ethnic groups in the southern part of Brazilian Amazonia) have realized that they had better work out a defense strategy based on not just bows and arrows—although that can sometimes prove a meaningful deterrent—but on opening up a dialogue with the whites and using their language and learning to work within their system.

They have banded together in associations and armed themselves with constitutionally recognized

rights. Their mission is to safeguard their material and spiritual heritage. This is clearly the most significant turn of events we confront as we approach the 21st century.

The Problem of Initiating a Dialogue Between Two Worlds

At the beginning of this century Indians had no constitutional rights in any republic along the Amazon, but the rubber scandal finally compelled the Brazilian government to create the Indian Protection Service in 1910. The first agency of its kind, it was designed to protect Indians from starvation, poverty, exploitation by whites, and introduced diseases. Its architect and guiding light, Colonel Cândido Mariano da Silva Rondon, a native Brazilian, was so popular that he was promoted to

Rondon escorted Theodore Roosevelt on a scientific expedition to Amazonia in 1913 and 1914. Roosevelt called him a "gallant officer, a high-minded gentleman, and an intrepid explorer."

the rank of marshal a few years before his death in 1956 at the age of ninety. The watchword he bequeathed to Indian Protection Service agents—"Die if necessary, but never kill"—vanished with him. Created in all innocence as an agency of the Ministry of Agriculture, the service became mired in a series of scandals from which it never recovered. By executive order, it was superseded in 1972 by FUNAI (Fundaçao Nacional do Indio) and its operations placed under the jurisdiction of the Ministry of the Interior. That was a step in the right direction.

Most Amazonian countries have followed Brazil's lead. They have set up government agencies within their interior ministries to oversee Indian affairs, although within very different legislative parameters. Some recognize Indians as full-fledged nationals who enjoy the same rights and responsibilities as their fellow-citizens. Others—including Brazil, home to half of all Amazonian Indians—regard them as de

"The social structure, languages, beliefs, and traditions of Indians are hereby recognized, as are their natural rights to lands they have traditionally occupied. Water utilization, prospecting, and development of mineral resources may not be undertaken on indigenous lands unless authorized by the National Congress and after consultation with the affected communities. Lands traditionally occupied by Indians are inalienable, and the rights pertaining thereto indefeasible."

Article 266, New Constitution of Brazil June 1988

facto minors who do not have the right to vote and whose rights have to be mediated through their caretaker agency, FUNAI.

A Big Step Forward, Provided Brazil Enforces Its Own Laws

The constitution of June 1988 made no provision for Indian suffrage, an issue that has sparked controversy in Brazil among self-proclaimed champions of the Indian cause. Some denounce the omission as paternalistic. Others argue that the government cannot grant rights to those Indians who are more acclimatized to white culture and—a key distinction —who speak Portuguese, and at the same time withhold them from those who choose to stay in the forest. And they feel that all Indians have a right to equal protection against the unscrupulous adventurers always poised to plunder their lands.

What the new Brazilian constitution does recognize—not an inconsiderable concession—is their right to lands they have traditionally occupied and exclusive rights to profits generated by underground resources. However, Congress still has the authority to grant or deny companies permission to develop those resources.

Thus, throughout most of the Amazon region, organizers of Indian self-help groups are aware that the fundamental rights of their peoples to land, language, and culture have been unanimously recognized, at least on paper. As representatives of their interests, they must struggle to bridge the often considerable gap between law and enforcement, and to see to it that these lofty principles do not evaporate in the tropical air.

Are Forest-Dwelling Indians Doomed to Extinction?

Mutual-aid associations have sprung up in Amazonia at all levels of Indian society, from villages to tribes, nations, and countries.

The Indians have shown that they can sit down at a negotiating table with whites and push just as hard for their cultural rights as for their language and land, which goes to show (with all due respect to doomsayers) that integration with the modern world need not always lead to acculturation, that unfailing destroyer of human individuality. Culture is what cements individual Indians to their group, without which they would cease to exist. As long as they continue to press for these rights, their identity is safe.

Therefore, our reply to those who ask if the Indians are dying out is a fairly resounding "no" if they mean those peoples with representation, some of whom are still forest-dwellers and have only sporadic contact with the outside world. This includes fully half of the 800 to 900 thousand Indians who live in Amazonia proper. But what about the rest?

Planners of highways across Amazonia paid little heed to the socio-cultural balances they were bound to disturb. Beneath its apparent uniformity, Amazonia is divided into hunting, gathering, and tribal migration zones that have evolved over the centuries.

After Five Hundred Years Will the Saga of the Amazon End with the Murder of El Dorado?

Global awareness of the problems in Amazonia has created the beginnings of change. With international

efforts to preserve the rain forests ("the earth's lungs") and its denizens gaining momentum, hope lies on the horizon. Deforestation and pollution are being fought both locally and on the global scale, and innovative programs such as "debt for nature" swaps—in which industrialized countries are relieving debtor nations of some financial burden in exchange for local environmental protection programs and the creation of new preserves—are exploring new ground. Such efforts, however, will represent real hope for the future only if local authorities enforce the principles of ecology and preservation of indigenous people on all administrative levels. It must also be said that, under the pretext of patrolling the borders and preventing guerrilla movement and drug trafficking, the armed forces stationed in the Amazon frequently abuse their power and they, too, prey on the environment and the Indian communities.

The 1979 words of Darcy Ribeiro, Brazilian anthropologist and political activist, still resound: "I have failed to reach my goal as an anthropologist: to rescue the Indians of Brazil. That's right, simply rescue them. That is what I've spent the last thirty

years trying to do. I have failed. I wanted to rescue them from the atrocities that have spelled extermination for so many Indian peoples.... Rescue them from the resentment and dejection sown in their villages by missionaries, official protectors, scientists, and most of all the land-owners who in countless ways deprive them of their most basic right: the right to exist and remain as they are."

What will the future bring? As international attention focuses on preserving the Amazon rain forest and the people and animals who live there, some people see reason to hope that traditional ways of life will not be completely exterminated.

"We are the descendants of a noble people that lived in balance with nature and took care of the great western continent they called home. We have had to endure the wholesale squandering of our land and people."
Galibi Indian from Surinam

Jívaro

Caquetá

Putumayo

Marañón

Quito

ECUADOR

Ucayali

Amazon

Andean
Cordillera

Pacific
Ocean

PERU

La Condamine   Humboldt   Bonpland

VENEZUELA

COLOMBIA

Yanomami

Apaporis

*Amazon
Solimões*

**ARAWAK
AREA**

ukuna

Japurá

Omagua

Juitoto

Juruá

Purus

Amazonas State

Madre de Diós

Piedras

Beni

Acre

Paragua

San Martín

Atlantic Ocean

Belém

TUPI AREA

Tocantins

Paranaiba

GE AREA

Cayapo

Emerillon

CARIB AREA

Ilha de Marajó

Santarém

Tapajós

Amazon

Pará State

Iriri

Caraja

Xingu

Nambicuara

Teles Pires

Chavante

Bororo

he heat. An empty sky, a ripple on the water,

GUYANA
Orinoco
Branco
Negro
Amazon
Manaus
Madeira
Mundurucú
Parintintin
Juruena
Pareci
Aripuana
BRAZIL
Guaporé

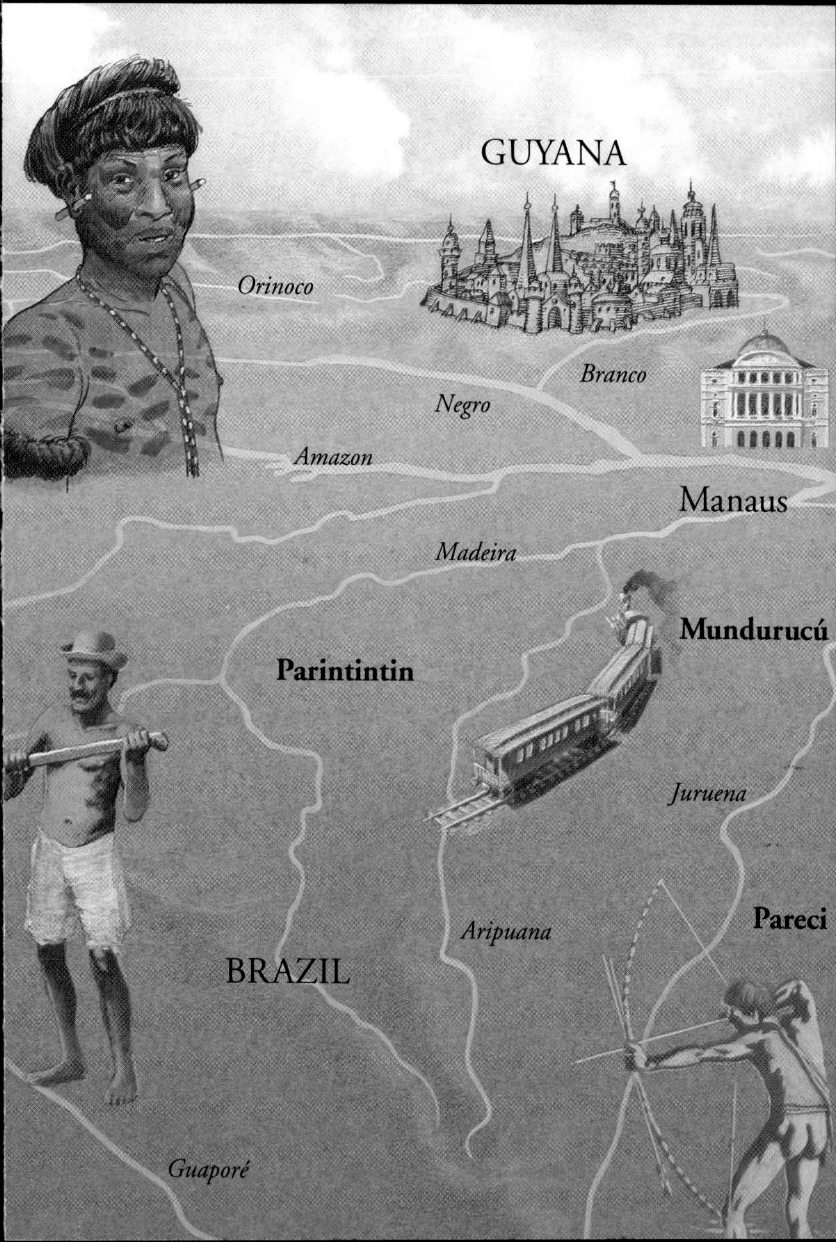

DOCUMENTS

Amazonia: mythic heart of Brazil, home of the "noble savage,"
land of mystery and dreams

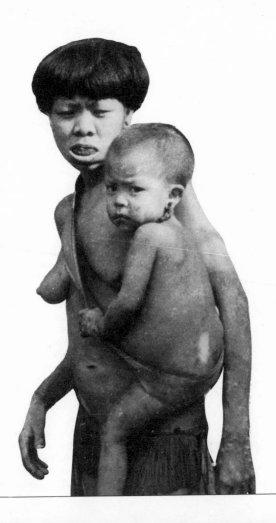

The Río de Orellana

On 7 June 1543 Francisco de Orellana appeared before the Council of the Indies to justify his conduct toward Gonzalo Pizarro. The authorities in Seville overlooked his "treason" and appointed him governor of the Amazonian territories. But his dream never came true.

The Prince [orders]: In view of the fact that you, Francisco de Orellana, owing to the desire which you have to [serve] His Majesty and to [see to it] that the Royal Crown of these realms is enhanced and that the peoples that are along the said river and in the lands come into [possession] of a knowledge of our holy Catholic faith, have requested to return to the said land to finish exploring it and to colonize it.... And [whereas] you have begged me to do you the favor of [conferring upon you] the title and power of governor over whatever [territory] you may explore on one of the banks of the said river, whichever one you may designate, I have ordered to be drawn up in your favor the following contract and articles of agreement:

First, that you be bound...to take over from these realms of Castile on the expedition of exploration and for the colonizing of the said land, which we have ordered to be called and named New Andalusia, three hundred men of Spanish nationality, one hundred as cavalrymen and two hundred as infantrymen, which seems to be a sufficiently large number and force for colonizing progressively and defending yourself and your men....

Furthermore, that you be under obligation to take along as many as eight clerics, any that may be given to you and may be designated by those who are members of our Council of the Indies, in order that they may take charge of the education and conversion of the natives of the said land;...

You likewise bind yourself to go in, for the purpose of carrying out the said exploration and colonizing, through the mouth of the river through which you came out, and to take over from these realms two caravels or ships which you are to send up the river, the one in advance of the other, just as soon as you shall go in through the said mouth and shall anchor in order to repair your outfit, and on board these [two ships there shall be] a few peacefully inclined persons and some clerics with the mission to take the necessary steps for persuading the natives that may be found to exist in the said land to adopt an attitude of peace....

In the belief that it is essential to the service of God our Lord, and by way of adding prestige to your person, we agree to give you the title of Governor and Captain-General over whatever you may explore on the said bank of the said river,...with a salary of five thousand ducats per year....

I furthermore do you the favor of one-twelfth of all the revenues and earned profits which His Majesty is to collect each year in the lands and provinces which you shall so explore and colonize in accordance with this agreement; which said favor I grant to you, for you and your heirs for all time.

Item, you shall take care to select, for the purpose of establishing the settlements which you are to establish, sites and regions where there shall be no infringement upon the rights and desires of the Indians of the said land; and in case they cannot be established, let it be taken with the consent of the said Indians, or with such

Ships such as the one at left sailed off in search of the land of the Amazons.

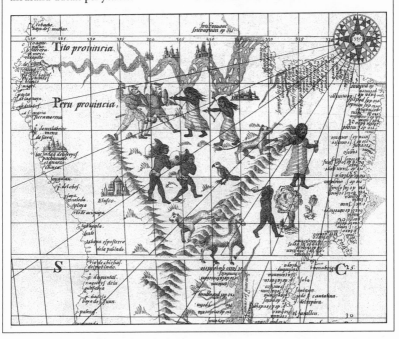

The conquistadors' dress was singularly unsuited for the rain forest.

circumspection as the inspector who is to go along with you to see how that which is stipulated is carried out, as well as the said clerics, shall think advisable.

Likewise, neither you nor any individual [among you] shall take away from the Indians any married woman or daughter, or any other woman at all, and that there not be taken away from them any gold or silver or cotton or feathers or stones or other article that [they] may possess, unless it be through bartering and upon the handing over to them of payment in the form of another article which is worth that, the barter goods and payment being effected in accordance with [the opinion] of the said inspector and clerics, under penalty of death and loss of one's goods; but we do give our consent that, when the food which you and the persons going with you are to take along shall be all used up, you be permitted to ask the said Indians for some with offers of barter; and whenever this may fail you, by means of entreaties and kind words and acts of persuasion you beg them for the said food, in such a way that at no time shall recourse be had to taking away from them by force, unless it be after all the said means shall have been tried out, as well as such other ones as the inspector and clerics and you may advise, for, in the event of your being in extreme need, the said food may be seized wherever it may be found.

Item, that in no way or manner is war to be waged against the said Indians, nor is any cause of such to be furnished, unless it be in defending yourself with that restraint which the situation requires. Rather we order that they be given to understand how we are sending you solely to teach them and instruct them, and not to fight, but to impart to them a knowledge of God and of our holy Catholic faith and [to inform] them of the obedience that they owe to us. And if by chance the Indians should turn out to be so haughty that, not heeding the advances and peace exhortations with which you shall have approached them, they will still come at you and attack you in a warlike fashion, you have no other means of escaping and defending yourselves against them, save by breaking with them, you shall follow this latter course with the greatest amount of restraint and moderation and with the least number of fatalities and injuries to them that is possible; and all the articles of wear and also objects of adornment that you may lay hands on, both by you and those who are to go along with you, you shall gather up, and you shall have them returned to the said Indians, telling them that you wish there had not been inflicted upon them the damage they shall have received, and that it was their fault for not having been willing to believe you, and that you are sending back to them those things which are theirs, because you have no inclination to kill them or maltreat them or take their belongings away from them, save a friendly understanding with them and redemption for them in the service of God and His Majesty; because, if you do this in this way, they will acquire great faith and confidence in what you shall have said and may say relative to this matter.

Likewise, any Spaniard whatsoever who may kill or wound any Indian shall be punished in conformity with the laws of these realms, without there being taken into consideration the fact that the delinquent is a Spaniard and the slain or wounded person an Indian.

And for the reason that, as you shall see by the said laws, it is the will of His Majesty that all the Indians come to be under our protection, in order that they may be spared and be instructed in the things pertaining to our holy Catholic faith, you must not allow any occasion

to arise serving as an excuse wherewith a Spaniard may hold Indians, or maltreat them, or prevent their becoming Christians, or take any object away from them except by bartering and according as and in the manner that it is stipulated.

Letters patent granted to
Francisco de Orellana for his
second expedition, 1544

The "Noble Savage"?

European attitudes toward Indian culture have diverged, at times considerably, along the long road from La Condamine to Jacques Lizot.

Yanomami children.

The Age of Reason and La Condamine

In order…to present an exact idea of the American people, almost as many descriptions are requisite as there are nations; however, as in Europe all nations, notwithstanding distinct languages, manners, and customs, have yet [something] in common to the eye of an Asiatic who examines them with attention, so do all the Americans of the different countries I had opportunity of noticing in the course of my travels, present features of resemblance, the one to the other, indeed (with exception of light shades of difference, scarcely to be distinguished by a passing observer), I fancied in all alike a similar base of character.

Insensibility among these people is generally prevalent, which, whether to be dignified by the name of apathy, or sunk in that of stupidity, I leave to the decision of others. Undoubtedly it is caused by the paucity of their ideas, which extend no farther than their wants. Voracious gluttons, where means of satiety exist; when want enforces sobriety they patiently bear with abstinence, and seem to be void of care. Pusillanimous and timid in extreme, unless when transported by drunkenness; inimical to toil; indifferent to every impulse of glory, honor, or gratitude; wholly engrossed and determined by the object of the moment, without concern for the future; destitute of foresight and reflection; and giving themselves up, when nothing prevents them, to a childish joy, which they manifest by leaping, and loud bursts of laughter, with no apparent object; they pass their lives without thought, and see old age advance, yet unremoved from childhood, and preserving all its faults.

Were this the picture merely of the Indians of some provinces of Peru, who may be regarded as slaves, the want of civilization might be ascribed to the degeneracy incident on their servile state; for the degradation to which slavery is capable of reducing man, is sufficiently exemplified in the present condition of the Greek nation. But the Americans of the country of the missions, and the savages free from all control of Europeans, showing themselves equally limited, not to say stupid, with the others, the reasoning mind cannot but feel humiliation, contemplating how little man, in a state of nature, and destitute of instruction and society, is removed in condition from beasts.

Charles-Marie de La Condamine
Abridged Narrative of Travels through the Interior of South America, 1747

The Happiness of Indian Life

When this article was written, in 1986, ethnologist Jacques Lizot had been living with the Yanomami for nineteen years.

He has their way of walking: the steady, decisive stride of the hunter. He speaks the same language. He laughs with them and knows how to make them laugh. Like them, he has a plug of tobacco inside his lip. He even sports the same little potbelly as his companions. And, he lives practically naked, as they do. Only, his loincloth is a swimsuit. Because he is a white man. The only white man ever to have lived among the warlike Yanomami Indians, in an isolated region of Venezuela that

shelters the headwaters of the Orinoco.

To look at his gaunt face, clear eyes, and straggly beard, you might mistake him for an explorer who has lost his way in the green maze of Amazonia. Not so. He is not a hostage of the vast rain forest. He is a voluntary exile who has spent the last nineteen years living another life. The life of an Indian from pre-Columbian times.

He was thirty years old and studying Islam in 1968. The anthropology laboratory of the Collège de France was looking for an ethnologist to accompany a one-year medical expedition among the Yanomami. Lizot has a will of his own. Shifting from Moslem civilizations to Amerindians was a challenge this maverick could not pass up. "I was supposed to be away for a year. But when the assignment was over, I realized that I'd need another year of fieldwork to get a handle on this culture that was so complex, so fundamentally alien to our own. You know what came next. Anyhow, it took five years for me really to be accepted in Yanomami society."

He greeted us beneath an awning covered with plaited palm leaves which forms a skirt around the earthen walls of his three-room "apartment" (kitchen, sleeping quarters, office). The Yanomami of Karohithéri—the little community of forty-odd souls he lives with—surrounded him like a *rara avis.* It was simple: All white men were, for them, "Lizoteri" (brethren of Lizot).

How ever did he manage to blend into a society so far removed from our own, in one of the planet's last unexplored havens of unspoiled life? The question amuses Lizot. "Actually, the problem is not to be accepted by the Yanomami, but to accept oneself in the field. At the most basic level, the Indians always accept you. The word they use to refer to themselves, *yanomami*, can be translated as 'human beings.' Which is tantamount to saying that, for them, outsiders, white people, belong to some nebulous species of subhumanity. We're human beings, all right, but of an inferior grade, something just for them to pilfer, plunder, and poke fun at. So, the problem is proving to them that you are their equal." A baptism of the jungle, ordeals by hunting and fishing, treks to test his endurance, inevitable rebuffs. The frail ethnologist's hide became weathered; so did his heart. A Robinson Crusoe without Friday, quarantined in the *shabano* (the huge circular open shed that serves as the communal shelter), he stood fast. In due course, that earned him a hearth and home (in the literal sense of the word) and an adopted family. So now he is allowed into the "circle of fire," which is the French title of his book on Yanomami society *(Tales of the Yanomami).*

The publication of *Le Cercle des feux* was hailed in 1976 as a milestone in anthropological research. The first thing that made the book unusual was the fact that it was written on the spot. While the iron was hot. That is what gives this book its warmth as it takes us into the world of Yanomami daily life.

It is a chronicle of the commonplace as well as the peculiar. Their funeral rites (they partake of stewed bananas mixed with the crushed bones of the dead). Their unbridled games of love (just one ground rule: everything that furthers pleasure is inherently good), but also the pangs of jealousy, the price they pay for this pagan sexual freedom. The tyrannical children, who are coddled little monarchs who grownups very seldom punish. The momentous initiation rites performed by shamans. The use of hallucinogens (derived from tree bark) to help them commune with the "moon spirit," the "whirlpool spirit," the "vulture spirit," and so forth. The gathering of medicinal and aphrodisiac plants. The plight of women in a warrior society. Hunting for wild pigs. Dancing, body painting, and self-adornment.

Lizot talks about the texture of the Yanomami's social life, their uninhibited morality, and the complexity of their religious world with fairness, without glossing over the cruelty of their civilization. "There is constant friction in the community; people come to blows over the slightest thing. But— how shall I put it—joyously!" He adds, "That is the keynote of this anti-'consumer society': joie de vivre."

You see, theirs is a community that does not know the meaning of private property, or power (there is no chief), or work as we know it (they put in two to three hours of work a day at the very most). Despite precarious living conditions, they have created a leisure society. "For example, they organize colossal battles with very hard clay balls, or fights with untipped arrows."

For all that, can it be said that paradise lies just across the Orinoco? Lizot does not believe in the myth of the noble savage. "Interacting with the Yanomami is both heartwarming and irritating. Without meaning to, they can really get on your nerves! They are tyrannical friends, forever touching you, foisting themselves on you, invading your house, talking to you whether you like it or not. If you get annoyed, they become sullen and grumpy."

Jacques Lizot in his "monkish" office.

Naturally bellicose, they are often at odds with neighboring groups, but warfare is part of their way of life. "In this case, their aim is not to conquer hunting grounds, but to punish offenses, avenge deaths, settle a blood debt. Of course, I keep out of internal feuds (even if it involves my own adopted family). However, within the group, I do advise restraint. By speaking their language and hunting as well as they do, I have earned their respect and the status of a wise man, admittedly due, for the most part, to my age. The Yanomami have consulted with me for years, to find out what I know about certain aspects of their own culture, because I have listened and learned, and knowledge is my stock-in-trade."

Lizot's "office" is monkish. A table fashioned from a door set flat on four posts, and a bench. But along a wall

there are shelves holding a good thousand books. To file his notes, Lizot even makes use of an Apple computer hooked up to a generator. Another luxury: a telescope. He is an avid stargazer and has shared this source of pleasure with the Yanomami.

Lizot has few illusions about the long-term fate of this last enclave of inviolate nature. Just recently, illicit mining concessions have attempted to encroach on Indian land. At Puerto Ayacho (the first built-up area, about 280 miles from the rain forest), Indian tribes are already being reduced to indigence, while farther south, the Yanomami of Brazil are being overrun by settlers. "The integration of primitive societies into our own is always traumatic. The rape of a culture. Even if the battle is lost, I am trying to delay the inevitable, to give the Yanomami time to learn to defend themselves. Based on my experience, I can't believe they are willing to swap their identity for a watch or a transistor radio."

Lizot, the naked ethnologist, gets out of his hammock to go tend his garden of banana trees, manioc, papayas, and pineapples. "I've even got some chickens, if you want an omelet...." Occasionally Lizot steals away from camp and cooks himself a tapir steak on the sly—rare! "The Yanomami only like meat when it's burnt to a crisp!"

Alain Kerjean and Jean-Paul Gibiat
Ça m'intéresse, January 1986

First Encounter with the Guaharibo

Lost in the Sierra Parima with Emiliano, their Maquiritare guide, Alain Gheerbrant and Pierre Gaisseau have just been surprised in their pajamas by a Guaharibo (Yanomami). Intrigued by this unexpected encounter, the Indian alerts the other members of his tribe.

If we were to make the slightest gesture of hostility that tensed bow would be loosed and the arrow would flash silently over the river and land in Pierre's chest. The next minute was of excessive length. We tried to smile, anxious to receive the delegate amiably.

The man in the canoe put down his paddle. It was not a well-made paddle in the form of a heart like those of the Maquiritares, but a plain piece of wood clumsily flattened at one end. He stared at us with wide-open eyes. It was an important moment not merely in our lives, but also in his. He wriggled and waved his free arm, gobbled like a turkey in his excitement, and tried to talk at the same time. He was so beside himself that he hardly seemed to know what he had come for; but after a while

Alain Gheerbrant and Pierre Gaissau.

he calmed down and delivered a long and vehement speech of which, of course, we did not understand a word.

Pierre had a packet of cigarettes in the pocket of his pajamas. Slowly and carefully, in order not to give the warrior on the other side of the river the slightest cause for alarm—the man still had his bow stretched and the arrow pointed toward us—Pierre took out a cigarette, lighted it and offered it to the man in the canoe.

"Ugh! Ugh!" said the savage, and taking the cigarette he made a clumsy attempt to smoke it, bit off part of it, and lost the rest in the river.

He began to bob up and down in excitement, laughing heartily and making signs with his free hand.

"Ugh! Ugh!" he exclaimed.

"What's he saying?" I asked Emiliano.

"He wants the whole pack, and the idiot doesn't even know how to smoke."

Emiliano had never been so indignant in his life, but Pierre handed over the pack.

"Ugh! Ugh!" said the Guaharibo.

I handed him a box of matches.

"Ugh! Ugh!" he exclaimed again.

What did he want now? He had thrown the cigarettes and the matches into the bottom of his canoe where they were already wet. We looked at him for a moment or two in silence. We were a little disconcerted. He began to wriggle and jump about even more than before. He got furious at our lack of understanding and pulled himself along the branch to get closer to us, stretching out his hand toward Pierre's leg. Finally we realized that he wanted our pajamas. We might have thought of that before. Pierre took off his jacket and handed it over. The anger immediately disappeared from the man's face and he began to laugh again.

"Ugh! Ugh!"

I took off my jacket and gave it to him. Then we took off our trousers. The warrior on the far side of the river had now relaxed his bow. The man in the boat bundled up our pajamas and continued to laugh heartily. He became almost delirious with joy. But we were now naked and we spread out our hands to indicate that we had nothing else we could give him. He seemed to understand and approve.

Now the moment had come to turn the tables, and Pierre and I took our cue energetically. We leaned forward toward the canoe shouting "Ugh! Ugh!" in concert. The fellow understood that too, and bending down he picked up a bow from the boards and handed it to us obediently.

"Ugh! Ugh!" we went on.

He picked up three arrows and handed them to us. The biggest was tipped with bamboo. It was a war head. The second was very much the same; it was an arrow for big-game hunting,

and the third was smaller, and bone tipped for hunting smaller game.

"Ugh! Ugh!" we continued to shout.

He raised his arms in the same sign as we had used. He, too, had nothing left to give, apart from our pajamas. Then it occurred to us that we were hungry. Catire had gone off with the last of our provisions. We had nothing left to eat. We hollowed our stomachs and beat a tattoo on them, shouting:

"Miam! Miam!"

He seemed to understand.

"Say 'bananas,'" Emiliano advised.

At that the savage made sweeping gestures with his hand, describing a circle round the forest and returning to us. Then he pointed to the sun and then to the east. Finally he let go of the branch to which he had been holding since the beginning of this memorable interview and pushed off his canoe and made his way toward his companion waiting on the rock.

Before long the canoe with the two savages in it disappeared round the river bend and we returned to our hammocks.

"Well, what did he say?" I asked Emiliano. "Are they going to bring us something to eat?"

"What a chance!" he replied gloomily. "He said they'd come back tomorrow with the whole tribe. But it won't be to bring us bananas, you can be sure of that. They'll take all they can find in the camp here and leave us without a stitch. And we'll be lucky if they don't kill us into the bargain."

He took his machete and the blanket we had given him a few days previously and went off to hide them. They were his most precious possessions.

Alain Gheerbrant
Journey to the Far Amazon, 1954

The Kayapo Indians Tend the Immense Field of Their Expertise

After spending five instructive years among the Kayapo, an interdisciplinary team of researchers concluded that physicians, agronomists, and botanists have much to learn from certain Indians along the Amazon.

We're only just now starting to realize that the Indians of the Amazonian rain forest of Brazil select seeds, domesticate insects, and practice a complex form of medicine. Dr. Darrell Posey has spent five years in the field in Pará, near the Guyana border; his research, conducted under the supervision of Kayapo Indians (the "Mébêngrôke" in their language) has turned up a vast body of knowledge that previous expeditions had largely overlooked. Funded by *National Geographic*, the National Science Foundation, and the World Wildlife Fund, the project ultimately aims to incorporate Kayapo expertise into the development of the region....

Consider this for starters: Farming with livestock in Amazonia impoverishes the soil in no time, whereas Mébêngrôke techniques make it more fertile. In fact, tracts of land formerly occupied by the Indians are very much in demand. The Kayapo create microzones of super-fertility and concoct a special mulch for each crop out of dozens of varieties of plant ash.

The Kayapo closely monitor the genetic types (phenotypes) of the plants they grow and select seeds according to hereditary characteristics (flavor, resistance to disease, etc.). Many researchers…do precisely the same thing in the lab. But for the Kayapo, every human kinship group is responsible for farming and improving just one type of crop. In addition, the Indians make the most of the interactions that occur in the rhizosphere, the still little understood world of roots. Certain plants secrete poisons underground to keep neighboring plants at bay. On the other hand, kindred species grow better at close quarters. The Kayapo know how to combine dozens of plants to create *ombiqwa otoro*, "friends that grow up together." This is something about which our agronomists, with their monoculture mentality, know virtually nothing.

Indian management of the rain forest is just as remarkable. The "Brazil nut" groves of Amazonia were thought to be self-sown. Not so: They were planted by the ancestors of living Kayapo, who carry on the tradition. The felling of gigantic trees to harvest honey from otherwise inaccessible hives, a practice for which they are often reproached, is actually a way of introducing hundreds of medicinal herbs as well as plants that attract game, thereby creating hunting reserves for the future. The Kayapo have at least one use for 98% of the 120 plants we counted in the clearings around the villages. In fact, they can differentiate among 250 types of dysentery, with a specific cure for each and every case—to the astonishment of pharmacists on the team.

Honey plays an important part in the life of the Mébêngrôke, who have their own way of classifying bees. On close inspection, the entomologists "discovered" nine stingless species. The Indians even practice biological pest control. The Kayapo surround their

Oyana Indians.

gardens with a hedge of a certain variety of banana tree that attracts wasps, the natural enemies of leaf-eating ants. Generally speaking, parasites are controlled by luring organisms that feed on them. When determining the location of fishing grounds, they defer above all to the territory of the *mry-kaak*. This 65-foot-long eel, which lurks deep in spawning grounds, sends out electric shocks that can be felt 1500 feet away. The Kayapo steer clear of waters that shelter the immature fish this monster is known to feed on.

How did all this knowledge slip by unnoticed? "As a rule," Dr. Posey tells us, "investigators are reluctant to let informants guide their research in ways that seem logical to *them*, and in areas of the Indians' own choosing.

Researchers end up conducting validity checks in just one category of Indian studies and publish gratuitous lists of Indian vocabulary. Very few biologists get the chance to learn the Indian languages that would allow them to do meaningful fieldwork."

This is an ongoing project. In 1986 the team documented 600 animals and 185 plants and their uses and analyzed 200 soil samples as part of a study of traditional Indian crop rotation over a twenty-year period. Since then, research has focused on the rainy season, collecting parasitic insects at night, and studying various ecozones in the rain forest once thought to occur naturally, but which the Indians actually created.

Marie-Paule Nougaret
Libération, 21 December 1987

Fear

The Green Hell was equally agonizing for a young explorer, a society woman, and a traveling botanist.

A Society Woman Lost in the Rain Forest

In 1767 Madame Godin des Odonnais left Peru to join her husband in Cayenne. She started down the Amazon with a group of people. She was to be the sole survivor of the expedition.

The following morning the two Indians had vanished; the ill-fated band re-embarked without a guide, and the first day passed without incident. Around noon the following day, they came upon a dinghy that had put in at a little landing near a native hut fashioned from tressed foliage. They found a convalescing Indian who agreed to go with them and man the helm. The third day, as he was attempting to retrieve Mr. R.'s hat, which had dropped into the water, the Indian himself fell overboard; he did not have the strength to climb back in and drowned. There the boat was, without a helmsman, left to be steered by people who knew nothing whatever of seamanship. As a result, it was soon flooded, which forced them to make landfall and build a hut. Andoas lay no more than five or six days away. Mr. R. volunteered to go ahead and left with another Frenchman in his party and Mme. Godin's faithful Negro, who was to assist them at her request. Mr. R. made a point of taking his belongings with him. I have since reproached my wife for not having also sent one of her brothers with Mr. R. to seek help at Andoas. She answered that neither one wished to board the boat after the accident that had befallen them.... As

A 19th-century view of virgin rain forest.

he left, Mr. R. promised Mme. Godin and her brothers that they would receive a boat and some Indians within a fortnight. A fortnight came and went, and twenty-five days later they were still waiting; having given up hope, they built a raft and climbed onto it with some provisions and belongings. They were equally inept at steering this raft, which ran into a submerged bough and capsized: belongings lost, everyone in the water. No one perished, owing to the narrowness of the river at this spot. Madame Godin went under twice, but was rescued by her brothers. Reduced to an even unhappier condition than before, they all decided to proceed along the river bank on foot.

And what an undertaking it was! As you know, Sir, the banks of this river are lined with woods that are thick with grasses, tropical creepers, and shrubbery, where clearing a path requires a bush hook and a great deal of time. They returned to their hut, gathered up the provisions they had left there, and set out again on foot. As they made their way along the river bank, they noticed that its loops and bends were adding considerably to their route; they went into the forest to avoid them and got lost in just a few days. Tired of walking for so long in a forest that was so rough and difficult even for the experienced, their feet wounded by brambles and thornbushes, their provisions used up, suffering from extreme thirst, they had no recourse but to eat seeds, wild fruit, and cabbage palms. Finally, exhausted from hunger, thirst, and weariness, they ran out of strength; they succumbed and sank to

the ground, unable to get back up. There they awaited their final moments; within three to four days, one after another, they breathed their last. Madame Godin, stretched out alongside her brothers and the other corpses, stayed put twice twenty-four hours, dazed, bewildered, dumbfounded, and yet racked by burning thirst. At last, Providence, intent on preserving her, gave her the will and the strength to crawl along and go looking for the salvation that awaited her. She was unshod, half-naked; two mantillas and a nightdress, which the brambles had torn to shreds, barely covered her; she cut her brothers' shoes off their feet and fastened the soles to her own....

How could a woman in this state of exhaustion and privation, who had been coddled since birth and was now in the direst of straits, cling to life even for four days? She assured me that she spent ten days by herself in the woods, two of them beside her deceased brothers and awaiting her own death.... On her second day of

Indians welcoming Mme. des Odonnais.

walking, which could not have taken her very far, she found some water and, during the next few days, some wild fruit and green eggs with which she was unfamiliar.... Her esophagus had grown so narrow from lack of food, she could hardly swallow them. Those she chanced to find along the way were enough to sustain that living skeleton. It was time for help to appear.

If you were to read in a novel about a frail woman, accustomed to enjoying all the comforts of life, who was cast into a river and pulled out half-drowned only to disappear into a pathless forest, walk for several weeks, and lose her way; who endured hunger, thirst, and fatigue to the point of exhaustion; who watched as her two brothers, who were far more able-bodied than she, died, followed by the three young women in her service and the young valet of the physician who had gone ahead; who survived this catastrophe; who spent two days and two nights by herself among these corpses in a land abounding in tigers and a great many very dangerous snakes, none of which she had encountered before; who rose to her feet, set out again all in tatters, and wandered aimlessly in the forest until, on the eighth day, she found herself on the banks of the Bobonafa—you would accuse the author of the novel of implausibility.

Letter from Monsieur Godin des Odonnais to Monsieur de La Condamine, 1773

The Sierra Parima

"The Sierra Parima is an impenetrable green hell." We were first told this in Paris, then in Caracas, and finally in Bogotá. "The Sierra Parima is an absolutely impenetrable green hell."

We were reassured by all the officials, colonists, rubber seekers, diamond seekers, gold seekers and wood cutters of Puerto Ayacucho.

The climate is quite sufficient to discourage most people, and some who are prepared to put up with that cannot face the super-abundance of mosquitoes and savage beasts of the upper Orinoco; while the rest, who do not fear either the climate or the wild beasts and know how to protect themselves against the mosquitoes, give up in face of the men of the mountains. "Guaharibos," they said sagely, putting their glasses down onto the table and nodding their heads. What they said was enough to damp the ardor of the most enthusiastic explorers, but we had already heard so much of it during the past six months since we had first descended the Cordilleras of the Andes, in fact for the past year since we first left Europe, that we were immune.

The two peoples known to exist in

Hauling a canoe through the Green Hell.

"the green hell" are the Maquiritares and the Guaharibos. The latter have made themselves feared and detested, while the former, on the contrary, enjoy the esteem of everyone, not only in Puerto Ayacucho but throughout the whole Orinoco area through which we passed. They are hardy and industrious, we were told, and in all the work they do they display a level of civilization infinitely more advanced than that of any Indian tribe we had met so far: Guahibos, Piapicos, or Piaroas. Certain groups of these Maquiritares living along the higher tributaries of the Orinoco maintain regular relations with the colonists and the rubber seekers of the forest, hiring them their services from time to time, as the Piaroas do too, and there is unanimous praise for the Maquiritares. The others, the majority of the tribe, still live around

the sources of the rivers which flow down from the Parima, going about naked, bedaubed with paint, and wearing feathers according to their ancient customs. But they have never at any time shown any hostility toward the rare white men who have fallen in with them in the course of their journeyings.

"The Indians you have met are poor, backward people," we were told. "You must go and see the Maquiritares; they're quite different. They know how to weave fine hammocks and to make wickerwork baskets and so on, ornamented with designs and patterns of animals and men, arabesques and decorative borders. They can dance and they have beautiful decorations of feathers. The men are armed with bows and arrows, blowpipes and impressive cudgels. The women make decorative pubic girdles ornamented with the colored glass beadwork introduced at the time of the Spaniards. They build immense clay huts with proper doors and windows, and they are the greatest hunters in the whole of America. They lack nothing and they make the best cassava loaves you can possibly imagine, every bit as good as wheat bread."

Thus although the Sierra Parima was unexplored, everyone knew the Maquiritares. The Sierra Parima was a green hell, but the land of the Maquiritares was described to us as a paradise of savages. More than once we asked ourselves, during the few days we spent in Puerto Ayacucho before launching out on our great adventure, whether all those people with whom we ate or drank beer were talking about the same thing.

But while what we heard about the Maquiritares was most reassuring, what we were told about their neighbors the

Guaharibos was certainly not. This tribe lived in the heart of the Parima and were the masters of the Orinoco sources, which still remained unknown after expeditions from all corners of the world had attempted to reach them. The Guaharibos were cannibals still. They killed and ate men. They were troglodytes who had remained on earth by an anthropological anachronism. The mention of their name was invariably followed by a long silence even among the most scarred and weather-beaten of the adventurers we met....

Alain Gheerbrant
Journey to the Far Amazon, 1954

Excursion into the Pará Region

Botanist C. F. P. von Martius and zoologist J. B. von Spix spent the years 1817–20 in Brazil. No one before them had so closely scrutinized the natural history of Amazonia. Upon their return, von Martius was appointed director of the botanical garden in Munich.

I turned away from the river bank and headed for the interior. First I had to make my way through a dense forest that seemed most inhospitable and showed signs of serious flooding. The tree trunks emerged from a clinging muck, then flared out into a lofty canopy of unevenly distributed boughs; water dripped unceasingly from thick leaves overgrown with moss and tropical creepers, and a layer of air permeated with decay hung motionless upon the damp, slippery ground, which was all but stripped of grass and shrubbery. The Brazilians call this forest *alagadisso;* in the Gê language it is called *gabo.* It is home to the cacao-tree, a few specimens of which I found growing wild, others planted in rows in

a *cacaol.* This tree does not reach an extraordinary height, nor do its branches achieve great breadth, because it bears its large, heavy fruit only on the trunk and principal boughs. Thus, seen from afar, these plantings suggest lanes of luxuriant, but carefully pruned linden trees.

Emerging from this *alagadisso,* I reached a higher area that was dry and treeless, the ground of which was covered with a cheerful carpet of grass. Nothing can compare with the silence that hangs over these inviting glades. While not a breath of air bestirs the mute, mournful, gloomy forest surrounding them, the warm rays of the sun spread all their brilliance upon the flowers, attracting countless butterflies, dragonflies, and hummingbirds that indulge in carefree sport. This spectacle was new to me, and I was immersed in it for quite some time, when suddenly the long shadows a few scattered *inajá* palms *(Maximiliana regia)* cast on the clearings reminded me that night would soon be falling and it was time I started out on my return trip. Just the same, before doing so I wanted to get a closer look at a nearby dip in the ground toward which I had now and then seen flocks of coots and ducks taking wing. I followed a shallow, water-filled ditch and soon found myself in front of a little pool of crystal-clear water surrounded by broad-leaved rushes and huge arum stems. How surprised I was to see that it was a bird pond, not unlike the memorable one along the Río de San Francisco! Here, too, the feathered kingdom represented all life— only smaller in size and less boisterous.

I then decided to head back to the river bank; but I soon got lost in the meandering waterways, the dense thickets lining them, and the narrow expanses of virgin forest that stretched out in various directions. The harder I tried to find my way, the more everything around me seemed to grow hostile and chaotic. The joys of that agreeable contemplation of nature were replaced by terror; for I came to a swampy area where I found myself surrounded by impenetrable groves of prickly palms *(Bactris marajá)*, where tacky arrowroot bushes became entangled ever more inextricably about me, where the broad-leaved heliconias on which I was trying to gain a foothold concealed a branch of deep water, and where, when I froze and strained my ears, I thought I heard the call of crocodiles, sure of their prey, on their way to make a meal of a stray traveler. Then, to my great horror, I realized that I had wandered into one of those suspicious ponds *(mondogos)* that the Indians themselves make a point of shunning because they are considered deadly labyrinths and thought to harbor dangerous animals. It was starting to get dark and, as I was unarmed, I had no alternative but to keep still and call for help by shouting and drumming incessantly on the tin canisters I used for gathering plant specimens.

After conducting myself thus for quite some time, to no avail, I clambered up the trunk of a *jubatí* palm *(Sagus taedigera)*, several footstalks of which formed a kind of stairway. I was surely safe from wild animals in the thick branches of this tree, but great care had to be taken not to get pricked by the spikes of the erect stalks upon which I was resting. Night gradually fell and myriads of stars began to shine overhead; but on that particular day I was in no condition to be uplifted and soothed by stargazing; instead I indulged the hope that my failure to return by that unusual hour would prompt my traveling companions to come looking for me.

Dr. Spix had, in fact, sent some Indians to track me down. Before long, several shots rang out, and I called out repeatedly in an attempt to answer back. At last I detected two moving lights that were making their way, albeit circuitously, in my direction. Two men from the *engenho* finally freed me from this terrible predicament and, displaying a thorough knowledge of the area, escorted me back to my anxious companions. The route they took was no less fraught with danger, for the torches they were carrying, made from the wood of the *jubatí* palm, only dimly lit the path, which was quite overgrown with bulrushes, reeds, and groves of marsh palms, the thorns of which had left my body bleeding all over.

When we got back to the *Rossinha* the following morning, we found, to our delight, quite a few letters from our native land waiting for us. Our very kind friend, R. Hesketh, had forwarded them from the Maranhão via the postman, who had made the grueling and hazardous trip in two weeks. They contained, among other things, instructions to set our return to Europe for the summer of 1820, thus confirming the plan already decided upon. By the same token, however, that left us little time to sail back up the Amazon, and our stay in Pará could be prolonged only until such time as preparations for that voyage could be completed.

Dr. J. B. von Spix and Dr. C. F. P. von Martius, *Reise in Brasilien auf Befehl Sr. Majestät Maximilian Joseph I,* 1831

The World of Dreams

For the Indians, there is no gap, no distinction, between the real world and the world of dreams, day and night, the seen and the unseen. Everything is equally real, eyes open or shut. Indians, like Alice, find it natural to step through the looking-glass of surface reality, although the passage is not always a peaceful one. There is much to learn from the imaginary world, but it has a dark side, too.

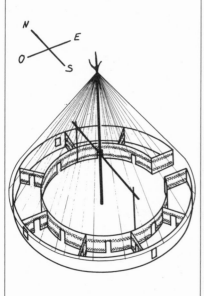

Genesis According to the Kogui Indians

In the beginning was the sea.
Everything was dark.
There was neither a sun, nor a moon,
  nor people, nor animals, nor plants.
The sea was everywhere. The sea was
  the mother.
The mother was neither a person, nor a
  thing, nor anything of any kind.
She was the spirit of what was to come.
She was thought and memory.
       As recorded by Alain Gheerbrant

Awena: Cosmic Myth of the Chimu Indians

The Chimu Indians of Colombia are a subgroup of the Choko Indians, who live on the west slope of the Andes.

When the girl had her first period, they confined her to a hut. When they went to see her two months later, she had grown so big they could not lift her up. When they returned a week after that, she had grown so much the hut could no longer hold her and it had to be pulled down. And still she grew, day by day. She toppled over and started to sink into the ground from her own weight and kept on sinking until she reached the other world. There she remains, beneath the earth, and when she stirs, her slightest movement causes the earth to shake. If she were to move a great deal, the world would burst to bits. Her name is Awena.

Awena's sister had a habit of bathing in a pond. The first time, she took an hour to bathe and returned home; the second time, she took two hours to bathe. When her parents went to see what was taking her so long, they found [the pond] filled with countless fish such as never had been seen before, which struck them as very odd. "Why are there so many fish?" they asked their daughter. Her answer was that they must not touch the fish in the pond.

One day, she went off to bathe and did not return. They went looking for her, only to discover two days later that she had turned into a fish below the waist. They tried to pull her out. "You cannot pull me from the water, and you never shall," said she. "For I am Benetenabe, mother of fish."

A view of the virgin rain forest, c. 1840.

That is why there are fish; had this not happened, there wouldn't be any. It is she who taught humans that her sister lived underground and that whenever she moved, the earth shook.

The two sisters never came back; and that is why menstruating women are no longer confined.

Chimu myth,
as recorded by Milciades Chaves

Chimila Shamans

The Chimila Indians live in an isolated region of the Colombian rain forest between the lower Magdalena River and the Sierra Nevada de Santa Marta. Ethnologist Gerardo Reichel-Dolmatoff, who visited them in 1944, believed them to be of Amazonian origin.

There are good shamans and bad shamans. That is what people say, and it's the truth. Good shamans look after the sick and cause it to rain, and when they die, they are like us when we die.

Bad shamans act differently. They do not go away when they die. They come back to do harm; and because they cannot come back as men—they would be recognized—they come back as tigers. That is why, whenever people go into the woods and come upon a tiger, they ask themselves: Is it a tiger or a shaman?

One day, some men went off into the forest. By nightfall, they had reached a large, round dwelling.

"Let us sleep in this house," one of them said.

"We cannot sleep here," the others said. "There is a man buried in this house."

The man went in anyway and began to sleep. The others stayed outdoors.

In the middle of the night, a big tiger appeared and killed the man who was asleep in the house.

"The man buried here is a bad shaman," the others said.

And they all ran away.

Recorded by
Gerardo Reichel-Dolmatoff

In Search of the "Nohotipe"

Helena Valero, the daughter of poor peasants who lived on a tributary of the Río Negro, was kidnapped by Indians at the age of eleven. She lived among various tribes, notably the Yanomami, for twenty-two years. In 1962 she told the story of her adventure to Ettore Biocca, who was on an expedition in Brazil at the time.

In the *shapuno* there was a sick woman. The old *shapori* [mythological serpent] had tried to cure her by sucking her and chanting their songs. They had said that the woman's *nohotipe* [spirit] had fled and that this was why she was so ill. That illness was *noreshi*. The woman was always complaining. Then they built on the compound of the *shapuno* a kind of enormous cage about three feet high, fixing in the ground some thick sticks and tying others over the top: it was the harpy's nest. Some men painted themselves black around the eyes, around the mouth, on the chest, on the legs; they entwined long *assai* leaves in their hair and hung them behind their heads like a tuft: they said that thus they were imitating the harpies, those big birds. Others painted themselves black around the mouth and the eyes, and on the legs: they were the monkeys.

In the afternoon, after three o'clock, they nearly all went outside to look for the *nohotipe*. The harpies with their cry, *fio, fio*...with leafy branches under their arms, beat their arms as if they were wings. The sick woman had stayed with a few men. At the big entrance to the *shapuno* a woman was answering the cries made from far away by those who had gone into the wood to search for the soul: "Look here, here is our home." Those who were pretending to be monkeys were shouting, jumping, waving the branches which they had in their hands. Those who were painted like otters were repeating the otter's cry. Even the children were following the others, painted like little falcons. The *tushaua* had said: "You will be falcons which look down from above and are the cleverest at finding; you monkeys, look among the branches." The women swept the branches along the ground like brooms. They think that they can find the *nohotipe* and thus drive it towards the *shapuno.* Many women carried their babies before them slung from their necks, because they were afraid that if they left them in the *shapuno* they too might have lost the *nohotipe.* After they had gone round an area where they thought the soul might have stayed, they went back into the *shapuno.* They passed round all the braziers and, with the branches, swept under the hammocks, in the corners, and they scattered the fire; then they again went outside the *shapuno.* They once more went right round it; when they came inside again, the most important Shapori said: "The soul is weeping in that place where we went that time." They all ran in that direction.

The sick woman did not improve: then they lifted her on their shoulders and carried her outside to look for the soul and to put it back in her. At length they returned inside the *shapuno* and one man squatted on that enormous cage which they had prepared: then another one jumped up on it, then another: they were the harpies and the monkeys. They also put the sick woman in their midst and, with the branches, began to strike her on the face. They thought that thus the *nohotipe* would more easily re-enter the body.

The monkeys stayed on the edges of the cage, jumping and shouting *eih, eih...,* while the harpies shouted *fio, fio*...and beat their wings. The women, the boys and all, as they came back, threw over the big cage the branches which they had in their hands. They say that that big cage, with the branches over it, is the harpy's nest. They all squatted over it. They turned the sick woman round and lifted her up; the harpies went *tak, tak*...beating upon the sick woman's body as if they were killing ants. According to them ants had entered into the *nohotipe* when it was lost in the wood.

At last a woman brought water in a *cuia* and some leaves which sent out a very strong odor. They are leaves which grow over the nests of certain ants called *kuna kuna.* Then they rubbed these leaves hard in the water and drew them over the sick woman's body and head. Slowly the woman began to improve: no more saliva came out of her mouth, nor did she groan any more.

They also believe that a man's soul is that great bird the harpy. When a man is ill, they say: "Perhaps he has fallen out of the nest, and cannot fly; that is why he is ill."

Ettore Biocca
Yanoáma, 1965

Images of Amazonia in Literature

The mysterious, magical, and impenetrable rain forest: Amazonia can inspire intense lyricism, but also nostalgia and near-disillusionment. "Final page of the unwritten Genesis…," as Euclides da Cunha put it in the early 1900s. Literature was, and remains, our window on a fascinating—and often disappointing—place. Human beings are intruders here, prey to their own frenzied imaginations.

Amazonia, Birthplace of Macounaíma

At the time of the Surrealist movement poets and writers looked to Amazonia, the mythic heart of Brazil, for them the true Brazil. In 1928 Mario de Andrade wrote about Macounaíma, the prototypical Brazilian hero, and his adventures in the jungle. His book begins with a description of Macounaíma's childhood.

In a far corner of Northern Brazil, at an hour when so deep a hush had fallen on the virgin forest that the brawling of the Uraricoera River could be heard, an Indian woman of the Tapanhuma tribe gave birth to an unlovely son, sired by the Terror of the Night. This child was an oddity, his skin black as calcined ivory. They named him Macunaíma; and he was to become a popular hero.

Even in his childhood this youngster did flabbergasting things. He passed the first six years of his life without talking. If anyone tried to make him speak he would exclaim, "Aw! What a…life!" but nothing more. He used to keep in a corner of the communal hut, climbing onto the sleeping platform made of trunks of the rasp palm and watching the others work, particularly his two brothers, Maanape, already getting on in years, and Jiguê, who was in his prime. His favorite pastime was nipping off the heads of leaf-cutting ants. He spent most of his time lying about, but if he spied a coin, he would toddle off at once to get it. He would also rouse himself smartly when the whole family went down to bathe, naked, in the river. He liked to duck under the water and disappear; the women would shriek with amusement at the crabs they said must be living in the fresh water there.

In the hut, if one of the girls came to cuddle him, he'd put out his hand to fondle her charms and the girl would run away. As for the men, he spat in their faces. However, he respected his elders and followed with attention all the ritual dances of the tribe, with their songs and dances prescribed for birth and death, for coming of age, for fertility and harvest, for fun and for war.

On going to bed, he always forgot to pee before he climbed into his little hanging basket. As his mother's hammock was slung below his cradle, the hero flooded her…every night. Then he slept, kicking his legs in the air and dreaming of dirty words and fantastic naughtinesses.

During the women's midday chatter the talk was always about the hero's pranks. The women laughed knowingly, saying, "The little one's prickly prickle already has a point!" And in the tribal assembly, King Nagô declared that the hero had his head screwed on the right way….

There came a day when the four, following a trail through the forest far from any creek or pool, were suffering badly from thirst. There wasn't even a refreshing hog plum to be seen in the neighborhood; and Vei, her rays piercing through the foliage, harassed the wanderers without respite. They sweated along as if under a spell in which their bodies had been slicked with butternut oil. Suddenly Macunaíma halted, and with a great gesture wrenched them out of their sleepwalking. Not a sound could be heard, but Macunaíma whispered, "There's something there!"

They left the beautiful Iriqui sitting on the buttress of a great silk-cotton tree, prinking herself up, while they cautiously crept on. Vei, the Sun, was by now satisfied with the flogging her rays had bestowed on the backs of the three brothers, so that Macunaíma, scouting a league and a half ahead, stumbled in the gloom over a sleeping woman. By her withered right breast he saw at once that she was an Amazon, one of that tribe of women living without any men on the shores of the lake called Mirror of the Moon, fed by the river Nhamundá. She was Ci, Mother of the Forest. She was a fine-looking woman, though wasted by debauchery and painted in black patterns with genipapo dye.

The hero flung himself on top of her to make love. She rebuffed him, and while he was drawing out his rapier she stabbed him with her three-pronged lance. A terrific scrap took place; the forest canopy above echoed with the cries of the scuffling couple, causing the birds to shrivel up with fright. Macunaíma was getting the worst of it. He took a punch that made his nose bleed, and he had a deep gash in his buttocks from the trident. The Amazon hadn't even the tiniest scratch, while with each blow she struck she drew more blood from the hero, who was letting out such dreadful roars that the birds shrank in terror. At last, getting the wind up from being outmatched by this female warrior, the hero turned and fled, calling to his brothers, "Help! Help! I'm killing her!"

The brothers rushed up and grabbed Ci. Maanape tied her arms behind her back while Jiguê bashed her on the head with his redwood club, so that she fell helpless among the ferns growing from the litter on the forest floor. When she had stopped struggling, Macunaíma closed in and made love with the

Mother of the Forest. This was the signal for flocks of parakeets, a host of scarlet macaws and green Amazon parrots, a multitude of parrots and parrotlets of every kind, to converge overhead to salute Macunaíma, the new Emperor of the Virgin Forest.

The three brothers continued on their way, taking the new ladylove with them. They made a tour of the most celebrated places in Brazil's romances and fairy tales: they crossed the Township of Flowers, avoiding the River of Bitterness; they passed below the Falls of Felicity and took the Way of Pleasures, arriving at last at My Darling's Grove in the foothills of the mountains of Venezuela. It was thence that Macunaíma ruled over the whole of the mysterious forest while Ci, grasping her three-pointed lance, commanded the warrior-women taking part in forays.

The hero lived a tranquil life, happily lazing away the days in his hammock, killing sugar ants and knocking back foaming mugs of cassava beer; when he felt like singing, accompanying himself with the fitful twanging on his little rustic fiddle with its monkey-gut strings, woods resounded with delight, lulling to sleep all such pests as snakes, ticks, mosquitoes, ants and the mischievous spirits of the bush.

At night Ci would return bleeding from her wounds, and then, reeking with the balsam she smeared on them, she would climb into the hammock she herself had woven from her own hair to keep the hero from straying. The two of them made love, and made love again, giggling and teasing each other. They went on giggling, close together, for a long time.

Mario de Andrade
Macunaíma, 1928

Challenging the History Books

In his struggle to preserve the cultural identity of his native region—he was born in Manaus—Marcio Souza has written two defiant and provocative books that recapture the splendor and decadence of certain periods in the history of Amazonia: The Emperor of the Amazon *and* Mad Maria. Mad Maria *deals with the construction of the Madeira-Mamoré Railroad, which opened in 1912.*

The engineer in charge of the project was an American by the name of Collier.

In the darkness of a night denser than the metal she was made of, Collier visualized the locomotive as a person. Mad Maria—that's what the men had decided to call this machine that was working for them. For the engineer, there was something inconsistent about their choice of name. It really wasn't an appropriate name for a locomotive. In the Latin languages South Americans spoke, "locomotive" was a feminine noun, so it was easy to liken the machine to a woman. But in English— and the people who had christened it were English-speaking—it was a neuter noun. At first, Collier thought this could be put down to the fact that Americans were in the habit of naming hurricanes and typhoons after women. But the locomotive gave constant proof that there was nothing disastrous about her. By no means "mad," she discharged her duties—faithfully, in fact. For a woman, she bore up bravely, unfailingly, where rugged men had knuckled under. Like everything in this world, there was more to her inconsistencies than met the eye. In a way, with her whims and contempt, this locomotive held sway over all the men at the construction site. She was queen of a hive of degraded, defeated bees. She was always there, imperturbable, sure of her course, each day looking down at the men from her lofty machinery, licking the rails with her iron teeth. She was Mad Maria, the Iron Queen, Collier's unapproachable woman, who drank for him, not gin, but engine oil, who made love for all those men in her bed of mud. But nobody visualized these things; not one of the men stretched out in their hammocks in the monitored dormitories realized what her presence meant, except Collier the engineer. Only he understood that they were all just dreaming as they rolled out a carpet before her. A swarm of prix-fixe vagrants who fancied themselves in the shoes of Sir Walter Raleigh, spreading out their cloak on the mud, that she might pass by, haughty and undefiled, on her metal feet. Only pirates and ruffians, like Walter Raleigh in the flesh, could have pulled off such a gesture; likewise, only these down-and-outs from the four corners of the earth could have sacrificed their own lives to spread out a carpet for Mad Maria. She was there, as if asleep, while her most punctilious slave, Thomas, plunged deep inside her. Every now and then, Collier wondered if this queen could be loved by her subjects. No, he reckoned she couldn't, because the queen bee is not really loved by her workers. And she must have known that her indifference would be paid back in kind. Neither hate nor love: only the indifference with which her tattered subjects laid down her carpet, piece by piece, day after day. A gesture which, from a distance, might even have looked romantic.

The following day, Mad Maria, awe-inspiring, spouted plumes of smoke, and from a distance you could hear the grinding of her metallic sighs.

Marcio Souza
Mad Maria, 1985

Preserving a Myth: Indians and Literature

Darcy Ribeiro, a Brazilian ethnologist specializing in Amazonian tribes, has studied Indian life and written about Indian myths and legends. His novel Maíra *deals with the gradual extermination of the Indian world.*

Isaias, a young Indian man, is returning to his village after spending several years in Rome.

From way up here, as I wing my way west, I can see, etched into the ground, separated from the forest and ringed by little encampments, the village where I was born. The houses are big woven baskets fashioned from tree trunks still green and pliable, and covered with straw. The biggest one, the *baito*, was for many a year the cynosure of Padre Vecchio, who wouldn't rest until he'd built a chapel that was even bigger. But the cross never could compete with the *baito*'s crowning ornament: two whole seasoned tree trunks, roots exposed, lashed to the peak of the roof.

It must be pitch dark in my village now. Inside the houses, everyone's asleep in hammocks tied to posts in the wall and poles, forming little family clusters. The man's hammock below; his wife's above him and their children's above her. Underneath, to take the chill off the early morning air, some paltry embers are burning, casting a glow on nothing but the floor....

My forest is a world of tall, slender tree trunks thrusting straight out of the ground, climbing and climbing and unfurling only way up at the very top. Light streams in only where a lightning bolt has knocked down a tree, but the forest closes its wounds right away. Its natural state is a green, gloomy semidarkness, like a Romanesque cathedral. Moreover, it comes to life but twice a day: at daybreak and nightfall, when choruses of monkeys leap about in the branches and cry out at the top of their lungs, and all feathered creatures sing or coo, wheeling in their fear of the coming night or their joy at dawn. Two masses are celebrated in the virgin rain forest: one in the morning and one in the evening.

All of us Maíra people dread nightfall in the rain forest. When that happens, we hang our hammocks very close together and poke the fire, terror-stricken, waiting for time to pass as we slowly make our way through the dark tunnel that is a night in the forest. For hours we live in constant fear that someone might say something to remind us of the chilling stories of men who fell asleep in the forest and lost

A moment of rest on a rubber plantation.

their souls by turning into animals, and lived as animals forevermore.

From way up here, as I gaze, not at the forest but within myself, in my heart of hearts, I can see my world. My village, Maíra, comes into view as it once was, as I saw it so many years ago. I see it time and again, in every detail. I can even see it in ways people ordinarily can't, like the age-old arrangement of sides and clans. An invisible line cuts the village into halves, the East and the West. Each has its own clans, which must go looking for wives or husbands on the opposite side. This partitioning of the village into halves mirrors on land our concept of the world, always divided in two: day and night, light and dark, sun and moon, fire and water, red and blue, male and female, good and bad, ugly and beautiful. One side of the village [represents] day, light, sun, fire, yellow. That's home to my family, the Jaguars, as well as to many others. The other side is nocturnal, dark, lunar, aquatic, deep blue. That's where our relatives by marriage live, like the family my brothers-in-law belong to, the little Sparrowhawks, along with many other people. One side says the other is womanly, ugly, and bad. Which side has these flaws has yet to be decided. But as for me, in my heart of hearts, I feel the ones on the other side are the ones that are unmanly, bad, and ugly. If it were a debatable point, I'd come up with many arguments to support my position. In my heart, all of us Easterners are the best-looking, the strongest, the best at everything—except me.

Darcy Ribeiro
Maíra, 1983

Black Gold and the Downfall

The autobiographical novels of José Eustasio Rivera of Colombia and Ferreira de Castro of Portugal recall the splendor and cruelty of nature in Amazonia as well as the sorry plight of the caucheros *and* seringueiros, *who were enslaved to rubber.*

Through the lyrical and passionate words of Rivera (1888-1928) in La Vorágine, *we relive the days of the rubber slaves and the traders who exploited them.*

A *cauchero*'s what I've been, and a *cauchero*'s what I am! I have lived amid muddy swamps, in the loneliness of mountains, me and my team of malarial men, pricking the bark of trees that bleed white, like the gods.

A thousand leagues from the house where I was born, I have cursed memories, all painful: parents growing old in poverty, waiting to be supported by an absent son; sisters, winsome and marriageable, smiling at disappointment, with no change in fortune to look forward to, no brother to bring them the gold that will deliver them!

Often, as I drove my ax into the living trunk, I'd suddenly get the urge to fling in onto my own hand that touched coins it never kept: ill-fated, unproductive hand that doesn't steal, doesn't recoup; I've come within an inch of taking my own life. And to think that so many others, in this very forest, suffer from the same illness!

Just who was it that created this imbalance between reality and our ever-yearning souls? Why were we given wings in a vacuum? Poverty was our cruel stepmother, hope our tyrant. We turn our eyes heavenward, but it means having to stumble here on earth. Our spirit comes to grief for the sake of our wretched bellies. Mediocrity has bestowed on us the gift of anguish. Heroes of mediocrity, that's all we were!

Those who managed to catch a glimpse of a happy life couldn't afford to buy it. Those who went looking for a fiancée met with scorn. Those who dreamed of a wife settled for a mistress. Those who tried to raise themselves up sank back defeated in front of powerful men as indifferent and unmoved as these trees that watch us waste away from fever and hunger among the leeches and ants!

I tried to silence illusion, but an unknown force drove me beyond reality. I overshot happiness, like an arrow that's missed its target, utterly helpless to break the fatal momentum, its only destiny to fall back to earth! And that's what they called my *future*!

Unattainable dreams! Forsaken triumphs! Why is it you that haunt my memory, as if you were out to shame me! Just look at what this dreamer has been reduced to doing: injuring inert trees to line the pockets of those who do not dream, putting up

with contempt and rebuffs for a piece
of stale bread at nightfall!

Slave, bear your hardships without
complaint! Prisoner, abide your jail! You
know nothing of the torment of
roaming, of being released into the rain
forest, where huge rivers are pillars for
vaults of green. You know nothing of
the agony of the gloom, what it means
to look at sunlight shining on the
opposite shore, the one you'll never
reach! The chain gnawing at your
ankles is more merciful than the leeches
in these swamps; the guard harassing
you is less adamant than these trees that
silently watch over us!

I've got three hundred trees along my
estradas and it takes me nine days to
torture them. I pulled the lianas away
from them, and I cleared a path to each
and every one. As I range among the
cunning band of plants to cut down the
ones that no longer bleed, I sometimes
catch men mutilating trees and stealing
latex from other workers. We fight it out
tooth and nail and machete, and the
contested milk becomes tinged with
drops of red! So what if our veins add to
the sap! The *capataz* demands ten liters
a day, and the whip is a usurer that
never forgives!

What do I care if my fellow worker
in the gully next to mine is dying of
fever! I can see him there, stretched out
on the leaves, fidgeting to shoo away
the flies that prevent him from dying
in peace. Driven away by the stench,
I'll have to leave this place tomorrow,
but I'll make off with whatever latex
he's tapped, and that'll mean that
much less work for me! And when I
die, it'll be someone else's turn to so
the same to me. I did not steal for
my parents, but I'll steal all I can for
my executioners!

Seringueiro.

As I encircle the latex-oozing trunk
with my grooved *carana* to wring its
tragic tears into the cup, the cloud of
mosquitoes defending it is sucking my
blood, and the warm mist of the rain
forest is filling my eyes. Each of us, the
tree and I, has its torment; we both
shed tears as we face death and we fight
hand to hand until we die!

But I do not pity the tree that stands
there and doesn't protest. A quivering
of branches is its revolt, but that cannot
move me. Why doesn't the whole forest
roar and squash us like snakes, to
punish us for our base exploitation?
Sadness isn't what I feel here, but
despair! What I wouldn't give for a
buddy to conspire with! I'd join the
battle of the species, perish amid
cataclysms, watch cosmic forces at work!
What if Satan led this rebellion!…

A *cauchero*'s what I've been, and a
cauchero's what I am! And what my
hand has done to trees it can do to men!
José Eustasio Rivera
La Vorágine, 1934

The Force of the Jungle

*Alberto, a young Portuguese, has arrived
at Belém do Pará and signed on with a
rubber plantation ironically named
"Paradise." His discovery of the forest is
about to begin.*

It was a separate world, a world in the
making—one productive of great
surprises, but tyrannical, tyrannical.
Not one of its trees had ever given him
any suggestion of the beautiful or
inspired him with any sense of intimate
delight. Trees, as trees, did not even
exist. What existed was a tangled mass
of vegetation: mad, disordered,
voracious, possessed of the soul and
claws of some hungry wild beast. There
it was, a silent, cloaked sentinel,
arresting his every step, closing down all
tracks and paths, ready to imprison and
enslave him.

The huge green wall and the
advance-guard of shrubs and
undergrowth which would come and
grow around it would sprout again with
an absurd and maddening insistence
after being cut down by Firmino's
knife. The jungle would never forgive
the slice cut from it, and would not rest
until the clearance they had made in it
should have closed, once more,
engulfing the hut in undergrowth after
ten, twenty, or fifty—it mattered not in
how many years—but some day. It
might be through the rubber trees
becoming exhausted; it might be
through the invasion of savages who
carved up the planters; it might even be

through some more trivial reason: but
in the end it was bound to happen. The
threat lurked in the very air that one
breathed, in the earth that one trod
upon and in the water one drank; and
it would be put into practice inexorably,
because there it was only JUNGLE
that could impose its will and hold
despotic sway.

Men were mere puppets in the hands
of that unseen force—that force which
they so stupidly imagined they had
conquered from behind their shield of
ambition.
Ferreira de Castro
Jungle, 1935

In Search of the Picturesque

In 1929 Henri Michaux published
Ecuador, *the story of a young man
who embarks on a trip across the Andes,
the mountains of Ecuador, and the
forests of Brazil and finally reaches the
mouth of the Amazon. Noted en route:
nothing seems to lead anywhere in
particular.*

*Iquitos, Peru,
A Port on the Amazon
15 November*

Daily occurrences make for a hum-
drum life. It happens everywhere.
However, one man's daily occurrences
can prove frightfully disorienting to
others—namely, foreigners—who are
used to different daily occurrences, even
if natives find them ordinary, dull, and
monotonous in the extreme.

The *issang* is part of everyday life in
this land. You walk through the damp
grass. Before long, you're itching. The
next thing you know, twenty of them
are all over your feet, hard to see except
with a magnifying glass, specks that are
red, but pinker than blood.

Three weeks later, you are one big sore up to your knees, with twenty or so pustules 1½ cm. across.

You're driven to despair, you curse, you turn septic, you crave tigers, pumas—but all you get is daily occurrences.

Another part of everyday life: tiny mosquitoes. They hardly sting, but they'll light in your eyelashes and nowhere else, by the hundreds.

You crave boas, but all you get is daily occurrences.

Also, in the water you'll find a charming little fish as thick as a strand of wool yarn; it's pretty, transparent, gelatinous.

You go in for a dip, they come towards you and try to get inside you.

They'll delicately probe your most sensitive spots (they just love natural orifices), then suddenly can't think of anything else but getting out. They back up, but backing up also causes a pair of needle-like fins to rise automatically. The fish-turned-open-umbrella gets nervous and fidgety and as it tries to escape rips into you, causing innumerable hemorrhages.

Either you find some way to poison the fish, or you die.

But here's the most ordinary ending of all: As soon as even the faintest trace of blood spreads through the water, the *caneros* crowd towards you. They're no bigger than sardines, but voracious and strong. They can snap off a finger in a single bite. A 60-kilogram man or woman takes them about ten minutes.

A corpse has never been retrieved from the Amazon.

A corpse has never been found in the Amazon...

15 December
Pará
Mouth of the Amazon

Numerous narrow channels 1 to 2 kilometers wide, that's all.

Just where *is* the Amazon, you ask yourself, because you never see anything more than that.

You've got to climb. You've got to be in a plane. So I didn't see the Amazon. That's why I won't talk about it.

A young woman who was in our party came from Manaus, and that morning as she went into town with us and walked into the Great Park with its handsome plantings, she let out a sigh of relief.

"Ah, nature at last!" she said. And yet, she came from the forest....

That's because the equatorial forest on either side of the river is a terribly sullen thing....

Henri Michaux
Ecuador, 1929

The True Scale of the Amazon Could Not Be Appreciated Until the 20th Century

Blaise Cendrars traveled "into the virgin forest by ocean liner." Here, too, reality proved elusive.

And yet, the forest keeps on rolling by.

The liner is sailing up the middle of the river or hugging now one bank, now the other.

Beneath the canopy of giant trees, the pervasive, greenish semi-darkness is scarcely relieved by the flowering tropical creepers that hang from the tallest branches.

Set like jewels into the opaque water of the bights and coves are little ocher, yellow, or white beaches, always crescent-shaped and where an alligator

is often stretched out, motionless.

Everything is still except for an occasional gaudy macaw, a dazzling toucan, or a chattering parrot shooting past on its way from one bank to its cover of greenery on the other; or else a surprised little monkey, jumping from its hiding place, sliding down, and scurrying away into foliage that rustles for but an instant. Or, every now and then, a big blue butterfly they call the *pamplonera,* a member of the Morpho family, fluttering about the boat as if intoxicated.

Here and there, a highly trained eye can make out a swarm of hummingbirds, suspended like a sunbeam between two clumps of bamboo or hovering over blossoming equatorial Victorias—those giant water lillies whose leaves are thick disks that can grow up to two meters around— moving up and down like a cloud of diamonds; or it might spot in the murky water, or glimpse in an eddy, the diving body of the elusive "manate," that strange fish with udders and a big, moveable head, which grazes on spongy grass and which is also known as the "sea cow."

But these extraordinary apparitions

A steamship on the Amazon.

last but a split second. The river, the forest, the plants immediately close over them, hide their wildlife, keep their secret, protect their life.

Not one voice. Not one cry. Not one sound. Flowing water. The forest is close by, shimmering in the heat. An empty sky, a ripple on the water, the stirring of a distant treetop, the quivering of a leaf: everything is enigmatic.

It occurs to you that this 12,000-ton ocean liner, laden with people, cargo, and things European, sailing upstream into the virgin forest, its propellers and mighty bow churning up and cutting through the yellow waves of the Amazon, its twirls of black smoke clinging to the trunks of the fan palms, is not the least bit intrusive or unsettling, that it is of no account amid the magnificence of primeval nature. In short, that it is passing through unnoticed, like a mosquito or a mayfly....

Blaise Cendrars
True Stories: Into the Virgin Forest by Ocean Liner, 1936

Vanished into Thin Air

"When did you last see white men? How many autumns ago? Try to remember.... Have you ever heard anyone mention the names Fawcett, Redfern, Maufrais?" Everyone exploring the virgin (but nowadays much visited) rain forest of Amazonia asks the primitive Indians these questions. Because neither Fawcett's nor Redfern's death has ever been proven.

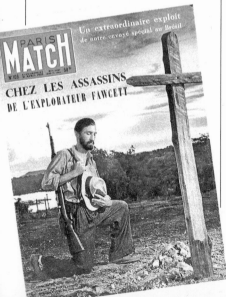

Un extraordinaire exploit de notre envoyé spécial au Brésil

CHEZ LES ASSASSINS DE L'EXPLORATEUR FAWCETT

Are they alive? Did they become the white gods of Indian tribes? Are they simply being held prisoner?

It has been twenty-five years since English colonel Percy H. Fawcett, his twenty-year-old son Jack, and their friend, twenty-year-old student Razor Rimmel, were "swallowed up" by the jungle of Mato Grosso, Brazil, where they were hoping to discover the ruins of a fabulous city, possibly treasure.

Twenty-three years ago, a young aviator, Paul Redfern, fell from his plane into the same forest; neither he nor his aircraft was ever found.

Just a few months ago, twenty-three-year-old Raymond Maufrais, a very inexperienced French explorer, vanished into the mountains of upper Maroni in French Guyana. His aged father, a pensioner from Toulon, went to Paris to question the last travelers to have met up with his son. He is still waiting for him....

"You Will Find a Fabulous City"

The adventure of Col. Fawcett and his son is legendary. In 1901 Percy Fawcett was a mystical student in love with geography. A married man and father, he left home to excavate sites in Bolivia and Brazil. After discovering very important relief carvings as fine as the ones in Memphis, he felt certain that the remains of a major unknown civilization lay hidden in the still unspoiled regions of the upper Tapajós and upper Xingu rivers. Captivated by the mystery of the Amazons, Percy Fawcett returned to the virgin forest in 1920 after being promoted to colonel on the battlefields of France. Malaria drove him away, but in 1925 he turned up at Cuyabá, a camp of gold and diamond miners in Mato Grosso. This

Percy H. Fawcett.

time his son, Jack, came with him. Percy Fawcett used to say that he was abiding by the wishes of an Indian witch doctor.

"You will find a fabulous city," the shaman had told him, "when your son is old enough to come back with you. You shall be taken prisoner, but by marrying he will set you free!"

It is because he believed in legends that Christopher Columbus discovered the New World. Percy Fawcett, his son Jack, and their friend Rimmel entered the jungle at Chepada. Three hundred kilometers into their trek, a Brazilian explorer provided them with two Indian guides and gave them a little dog that they promised to watch over like a fetish.

For a while, their campfires could be seen every night in the Sierra Azul,

where peaceful Indian tribes lived. In June 1925 the guides came back alone, bringing with them wonderful letters and film that Fawcett had committed to their care. Percy explained that increasingly dense jungle growth had made it impossible to clear a path with axes. He had built a canoe. His son, Rimmel, and he were traveling up the Río Koloseu, towards the settlements of the primitive Kalapalo Indians. A few days later, the little dog, covered with sores and frightened to death, wandered onto a loggers' ranch—alone.

The Wild Child

There are no cruel Indians—all explorers will back me up on that—only timorous men everywhere you go. At first, rumor had it that the three explorers had been poisoned. However, in 1925, the French explorer Courteville reported that he had met up with a white man suffering from malaria and total amnesia—possibly Percy Fawcett—near the San Rafael river. Again, it was Percy Fawcett a Swiss explorer claimed to have seen living among a barbaric tribe. He had a white beard, spoke English, was in excellent health; but when the European tried to get near him, the Indians stood in his way; they were holding him prisoner. According to Italian scientist Michele Trucchi, who also explored the region, Jack Fawcett and Rimmel had died; but Percy, desperate and suffering from leprosy, had stayed behind with the Indians and sworn never again to return to the civilized world. Brazilian ethnologist Willy Aureli, for his part, maintains that the sole survivor, Percy Fawcett, now rules over a tribe of cannibals.

Several adventurers and globetrotters

—such as Dyott, Petrulho, Fleming, and Oranio Fusani, head of the United Press in Rio de Janeiro—died in the forest looking for Fawcett. In 1934, another journalist, the Marquis of Winton, found the explorer's log book and some camera equipment. But nothing more could be learned because he, too, never came back. He was poisoned by Kalapalo Indians. In 1936 Rev. Leghters, corroborating a piece of information his associate, Tulla, had passed along back in 1926, reported that the Yananhaqua Indians, who lived near the Kalapalo, were looking after a blue-eyed white boy, the son of Jack Fawcett and his wife Alca, a maiden from their tribe. An expedition led by journalist Edmar Morel went looking for this child, named Dunpe, in 1945. He was adopted by Percy Fawcett's widow; today, he is twenty-five and studying in Brazil. The Indians told Morel that Rimmel had died of malaria and that Percy and Jack had been shot down by arrows. To this day, however, Percy's widow in London refuses to believe that her husband and son are dead!...

The Last Adventure of Raymond Maufrais

The name of a young French explorer, Raymond Maufrais, has since been added to those of Fawcett and Redfern.

A former parachutist and holder of the Croix de Guerre, Raymond Maufrais was a young journalist with a yen for adventure. In 1946 he took part in an expedition to Brazil. In November 1949 he contemplated the seeming

unachievable feat of reaching the distant Tumuc-Humac mountains of French Guyana alone, on foot, and carrying 30 kilograms of gear. There, according to a legend that had cost many men their lives for over four centuries, lay the fancied realm of a sovereign clad in pure gold who ruled over a fabulously wealthy people that lived in gold-covered houses. Raymond had no illusions as far as "El Dorado" [the golden king] was concerned, but he was intent on living a life of high adventure and on discovering, perhaps, the rich veins of gold that were known to exist in the region. He planned to publish the story of his upcoming journey, entitled "Adventures in the Tumuc-Humac Mountains," in *Sciences et Voyages.*

Five months later, a dozen Indians traveling up the Tamouri River came across his abandoned equipment, his rifle in particular, and log book. They notified Maripasouca police station, and the French authorities launched an investigation. Their findings did not bode well. They established that on 15

E xpedition on the Amazon

November Maufrais and his dog, Bobby, had reached what used to be a village of *balatistes* (balata-gum harvesters). On 15 January he made a raft out of tree trunks and cast off at a particularly turbulent spot in the river in hopes of reaching Bienvenue, a gold-mining station some forty-five kilometers away. Soon thereafter, the wreckage of his makeshift raft was found not far from his last known shelter.

They found his hammock still hanging beside a wooden table; on it there were some pieces of paper, an inkwell, a pen, and a half-rotted knapsack. The Indians and police followed the tracks of the unfortunate explorer into the rain forest but did not find his corpse. Since there are no primitive Indians in French Guyana, the investigators concluded that Raymond had most likely been eaten by wild animals.

"All the same, I think he's alive," his father maintains.

Dowsers have assured him that he is still roaming the Tumuc-Humac Mountains. And so the stories that Fawcett, Redfern, and he are still alive live on.

These three ghosts haunt the path to adventure that still lures many an explorer to the Amazon: in particular, Bertrand Flornoy, who has recently discovered the source of the mighty river, and Gheerbrant, Fichter, Matter, and Gaisseau, who have been following in the footsteps of La Condamine, d'Orbigny, Crevaux, and Condreau, serving science amid 200,000 Indians that are cut off from the outside world.

Henri Danjou
France-Soir, 8 January 1951

The Fabulous Bestiary

The Indians see no difference whatever between animal or plant spirits, which can appear in human guise, and themselves. Nineteenth-century naturalists saw a rare and priceless specimen as the future pride of European collections; the Indians saw it as the stray soul of one of their own people.

How Birds Acquired Their Colored Plumage

Men and birds joined forces to destroy the huge watersnake, which dragged all living creatures down to his lair. But the attackers took fright and cried off, one after the other, offering as their excuse that they could only fight on dry land. Finally the [cormorant] was brave enough to dive into the water; he inflicted a fatal wound on the monster…. The men succeeded in bringing the snake out of the water, where they killed it and removed its skin. The [cormorant] claimed the skin as the price of its victory. The Indian chiefs said ironically, "By all means! Just take it away!" "With pleasure," replied the [cormorant] as it signaled to the other birds. Together they swooped down and, each one taking a piece of the skin in its beak, flew off with it. The Indians were annoyed and… became the enemies of birds.

The birds retired to a quiet spot in order to share the skin. They agreed that each one should keep the part that was in its own beak. The skin was made up of marvelous colors—red, yellow, green, black, and white—and had markings no one had ever seen before. As soon as each bird was provided with the part to which it was entitled, the miracle happened: Until that time all birds had had dingy plumage, but now suddenly they became white, yellow, and blue.... The parrots were covered in green and red, and the macaws with red, purple, and gilded feathers, such as had never before been seen. The [cormorant], to which all the credit was due, was left with the head, which was black. But it said it was good enough for an old bird.

As told by Claude Lévi-Strauss
The Raw and the Cooked, 1964

Off the two of them went till they reached the river, and they started fishing on the beach. Then a big alligator emerged from the water, caught the man, and swallowed him—and his bow and arrows, too.

When he was in the alligator's belly, the man said, "I'm famished and there's nothing to eat. I'm thirsty and there's nothing to drink. I'd like to see light, and it's dark in here."

Just then he heard a monkey howling.

"If the monkeys are howling," he said, "it must be light!"

He took his arrow and started jabbing at the alligator's belly from inside.

The alligator came out of his hole and said, "Who's jabbing at me like that?"

The man kept on jabbing, again and again, and the alligator started running

The Man Who Dreamed of Alligators

"I had a dream about an alligator," a man said one day as he got out of bed.

"I dreamed I was walking along the beach and found a big alligator egg. I ate it. Now I'm afraid the alligator may come and eat *me*!

"Don't be a fool," his brother said. "Alligators are people like us. He's not going to eat you!"

Come evening, his brother said, "Let's go fishing."

"No," said the man. "I'm afraid of the alligator." But his brother insisted.

here, there, and everywhere in the river. He coughed so hard that he had to open his mouth. In no time the man placed his arrow crosswise to keep it from shutting, and out he darted. He fell onto the beach, half-dead.

That night, he woke up and headed back to his house. When he got there, the people were busy drinking *chicha*. His brother rose to greet him.

Then the man said, "That's what happens when you dream of alligators. But you wouldn't believe me!"

As told by Gerardo Reichel-Dolmatoff

The Anaconda

While poling steadily along under the lee of the left bank, one day Jack called out suddenly:—

"There's a dead alligator over there; let's get out of here."

I turned to look in the direction in which he had pointed. In a moment I saw his mistake. There lay in the mud and water, covered with flies, butter-flies, and insects of all sorts, the most colossal anaconda which ever my wildest dreams had conjured up. Ten or twelve feet of it lay stretched out on the bank in the mud; the rest of it lay in the clear shallow water, one loop of it under our canoe, its body as thick as a man's wrist. I have told the story of its length many times since, but scarcely ever have been believed. It measured fifty feet for a certainty, and probably nearer sixty. This I know from the position in which

it lay. Our canoe was a twenty-four footer; the snake's head was ten or twelve feet beyond the bow; its tail was a good four feet beyond the stern; the center of its body was looped up into a huge S, whose length was the length of our dug-out, and whose breadth was a good five feet....

I was in the stern where I couldn't reach the rifles, so I called out to Jack to shoot. He reached out for his weapon, but the noise he made in fumbling for it among the stores alarmed the snake. With one great swirl of the water that nearly wrecked us it vanished. The agility with which it moved was absolutely astounding in view of its great bulk, in striking contrast to the one we skinned. When I thought of how the latter's decapitated body had coiled round my legs and nearly broken them in the last contraction of its dying muscles, I wondered what would have happened to us had that huge beast in its headlong flight taken a turn round the canoe. How utterly helpless the mightiest of men would be in the coils of such a monster!

Fritz W. Up de Graff
Head-Hunters of the Amazon, 1923

The Gaze of the Scientist

Henry Walter Bates and Alfred Russel Wallace arrived in Pará on 28 May 1848. Bates stayed on for eleven years. When he got back to England, he met Darwin, who encouraged him to write the book that was to make him famous: The Naturalist on the River Amazons.

About midnight the wind, for which we had long been waiting, sprang up, the men weighed anchor, and we were soon fairly embarked on the Amazons. I rose long before sunrise, to see the great river

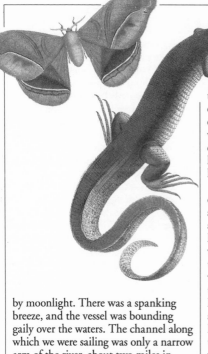

by moonlight. There was a spanking breeze, and the vessel was bounding gaily over the waters. The channel along which we were sailing was only a narrow arm of the river, about two miles in width: the total breadth at this point is more than twenty miles, but the stream is divided into three parts by a series of large islands. The river, notwithstanding this limitation of its breadth, had a most majestic appearance. It did not present that lake-like aspect which the waters of the Pará and Tocantins affect, but had all the swing, so to speak, of a vast flowing stream.... At daylight, on the sixth, a chain of blue hills, the Sierra de Almeyrim, appeared in the distance on the north bank of the river. The sight was most exhilarating after so long a sojourn in a flat country.... The hills, according to Von Martius, who landed here, are about 800 feet above the level of the river, and are thickly wooded to the summit. They commence on the east by a few low isolated and rounded elevations; but towards the west of the village, they assume the appearance of elongated ridges, which seem as if they had been planed down to a uniform height by some external force....

We used to make our halt in a small cleared place, tolerably free from ants and close to the water. Here we assembled after our toilsome morning's hunt in different directions through the woods, took our well-earned meal on the ground—two broad leaves of the wild banana serving us for a tablecloth—and rested for a couple of hours during the great heat of the afternoon.... A number of large, fat lizards two feet long, of a kind called by the natives Jacuarú *(Teius teguexim)* were always observed in the still hours of mid-day scampering with great clatter over the dead leaves, apparently in chase of each other.... The lazy flapping flight of large blue and black morpho butterflies high in the air, the hum of insects, and many inanimate sounds, contributed their share to the total impression this strange solitude produced. Heavy fruits from the crowns of trees which were mingled together at a giddy height overhead, fell now and then with a startling "plop" into the water. The breeze, not felt below, stirred in the topmost branches, setting the twisted and looped *sipós* in motion which creaked and groaned in a great variety of notes...

At Cametá I chanced to verify a fact

relating to the habits of a large hairy spider of the genus Mygale, in a manner worth recording.... The individual was nearly two inches in

length of body, but the legs expanded seven inches, and the entire body and legs were covered with coarse grey and reddish hairs. I was attracted by a movement of the monster on a tree-trunk; it was close beneath a deep crevice in the tree, across which was stretched a dense white web. The lower part of the web was broken, and two small birds, finches, were entangled in the pieces; they were about the size of the English siskin, and I judged the two to be male and female. One of them was quite dead, the other lay under the body of the spider not quite dead, and was smeared with the filthy liquor or saliva exuded by the monster. I drove away the spider and took the birds, but the second one soon died.... One day I saw the children belonging to an Indian family who collected for me with one of these monsters secured by a cord round its waist, by which they were leading it about the house as they would a dog....

On the sixth of October we left Ega

on a second excursion; the principal object being, this time, to search certain pools in the forest for young turtles. The exact situation of these hidden sheets of water is known only to a few practiced huntsmen; we took one of these men with us from Ega, a mameluco named Pedro, and on our way called at Shimuní for Daniel to serve as an additional guide.... When the net was formed into a circle, and the men had jumped in, an alligator was found to be enclosed. No one was alarmed, the only fear expressed being that the imprisoned beast would tear the net. First one shouted, "I have touched his head;" then another, "he has scratched my leg;" one of the men, a lanky Miránha, was thrown off his balance, and then there was no end to the laughter and shouting. At last a youth of about fourteen years of age, on my calling to him, from the bank, to do so, seized the reptile by the tail, and held him tightly until, a little resistance being overcome, he was able to bring it ashore. The net was opened, and the boy slowly dragged the dangerous but cowardly beast to land through the muddy water, a distance of about a hundred yards. Meantime, I had cut a strong pole from a tree, and as soon as the alligator was drawn to solid ground, gave him a smart rap with it on the crown of his head, which killed him instantly. It was good-sized individual; the jaws being considerably more than a foot long, and fully capable of snapping a man's leg in twain. The species was the large caiman, the Jacaré-uassú of the Amazonian Indians....

The natives at once despise and fear the great caiman. I once spent a month at Caicara, a village of semi-civilized Indians, about 20 miles west of Ega....

The river had sunk to a very low point, so that the port and bathing-place of the village now lay at the foot of a long sloping bank, and a large caiman made his appearance in the shallow and muddy water. We were all obliged to be very careful in taking our bath; most of the people simply using a calabash, pouring the water over themselves while standing on the brink. A large trading canoe, belonging to a Barra merchant named Soares, arrived at this time, and the Indian crew, as usual, spent the first day or two after their coming into port, in drunkenness and debauchery ashore. One of the men, during the greatest heat of the day, when almost every one was enjoying his afternoon's nap, took it into his head whilst in a tipsy state to go down alone to bathe. He was seen only by the Juiz de Paz, a feeble old man who was lying in his hammock, in the open veranda at the rear of his house on the top of the bank, and who shouted to the besotted Indian to beware of the alligator. Before he could repeat his warning, the man stumbled, and a pair of gaping jaws, appearing suddenly above the surface, seized him round the waist and drew him under the water. A cry of agony *"Ai Jesús!"* was the last sign made by the wretched victim.

Henry Walter Bates
The Naturalist on the River Amazons
1863

Amazonia Fever

The Great Brazilian Dream. Lungs of the world. Breadbasket of the planet. A fertile belly, source of all Brazilian optimism, vindication of Brazil's wait-and-see policies. "Out there," Vargas once said, "lies an unpeopled land for landless people."

Brazilians have "Amazon fever." A strange disease that has stricken an entire nation. It casts them, all agog, onto uncertain roads leading to that humid, mossy patch of green at the top of the country on the maps the Annuario Geographici do Sul publishes. They've all come down with it: losers from the big cities, have-nots from sprawling sugar plantations, outcasts of every persuasion and complexion, but also company boosters from Brasilia, politicians from São Paolo, illuminati from Bahia, even the Archbishop of Recife, who is convinced that "God is Amazonian."

"The future lies in Amazonia," economist Paul Ramos once claimed. "Why, if it were a nation, it would rank seventh in the world, just behind Australia and India. If all the trees in the rain forest were cut down, a third of all woodlands would vanish from the face of the earth. If you drained the Amazon and its tributaries, the world would lose one-fifth of its water. If…"

If…Hopes and dreams often hang on such words. "Tomorrow, comrade," goes a song they sing in the *favelas* (slums) of Rio. "Tomorrow you'll lend a helping hand to the weary, exhausted, starving Old World. To it you'll offer the riches of Amazonia. Tomorrow…"

Tomorrow Is Here

In 1960 forest-crushing monsters started cutting a swath eight meters wide through the jungle at the rate of six kilometers [3.7 miles] an hour. The backbone of Brazil, linking Brasilia and Belém, was in place, and through it

G old miners in Brazil.

surged hordes of new farmers eager to help themselves to the "green gold" that had been promised them. Before long they were lost inside their forest-tomb, cut off, digested by the bowels of nature. Occasionally you run into some of these wretched *caboclos* sitting motionless in front of their lopsided shanties on the riverbank, subsisting on a meager crop of papayas or bananas. The faces you see on these sullen loners register an undefinable something that immediately recalls the sadness of the Indian and the arrogance of the early *bandeirantes*.

In 1966 a second, highly publicized attempt with the launching of "Operation Amazonia." The Office of Amazonian Development (SUDAM) concocted a program bursting with generous incentives for investors (especially foreign ones); to show its good faith, it devised a "penetration scheme" and implemented it in record time. The next fifteen years witnessed the building of 15,000 kilometers [9300 miles] of railway lines, 3000 kilometers [1850 miles] of paved roads, 14,000 kilometers [8700 miles] of dirt roads, and the famous 4,300-kilometer [2700-mile] Trans-Amazon Highway, which crosses Brazil from Cruzeiro do Sul in the west to João Pessoa in the east.

The construction of the "big road" was an epic undertaking. Working themselves into a frenzy, Brazilians monitored its progress meter by meter and evaluated the efficiency of the bulldozers as they relentlessly knocked down trees, drove out monkeys, and marooned groups of primitive Indians on the highway embankment—stone-age tribes with no previous contact with the white man's world, and now sick,

uprooted alcoholics. From Guyana to Peru, Pôrto Velho to Manaus, Cuiabá to Santarém, the land was burned, cleared, despoiled.

It all came to naught. Of the 10,000-odd projects filed with SUDAM in 1966, a scant hundred or so actually got under way and only a tiny fraction proved successful. All that is left of the 120,000 square kilometers [46,300 square miles] of cleared forest is a handful of bits of land stingily worked by disillusioned *caboclos*. Moreover, in 1976, the government officially declared the operation a failure. Tax abatements for creating new development zones were eliminated. They started to encourage emigration, not immigration.

The Amazonian rain forest is not what people thought it was. It is an idol with feet of clay. It is the climate, not fertile soil, that makes it so lush. Itinerant slash-and-burn farming, the only kind feasible for its shallow, humus-poor earth, yields at the very most a few crops of manioc, cereals, rice, and tobacco. Within two seasons, the ground, played out, washed away by rains and high water, becomes totally barren. Turning it into productive land requires huge investments.

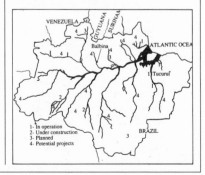

1 - In operation
2 - Under construction
3 - Planned
4 - Potential projects

"Success Stories" Are Not to Be Believed: They Are Often Shams

Case in point: the pepper-tree farm north of Santarém, the latest experiment on the part of a Japanese team, where every plant had to be rooted in a pot of prepared earth. Huge tracts of land in Mato Grosso, sown with fodder crops suitable for livestock. For local cattle-breeders. Ten million head in ten years. A success, they report to the ministry. "But most of all a success for the speculators who bought these uncharted parcels for nominal sums and triggered a full-blown, if artificial boom."

Prof. Oliveras Do Santos, a realist, points out to his students at the University of São Paulo that Amazonia is a come-on. A smokescreen the powers-that-be use to temporarily patch over the endemic ills from which the country suffers: poverty and hunger.

"There's a good reason for all this," he says. "In our country, hunger is profitable. It pays off by means of fraudulent economic plans, abortive growth projects, sham incentives to spur investment, and senseless, pie-in-the-sky development schemes. Hunger here is a source of profits, promotional fees, rents, dividends, interest, commissions generated by loan activity, and Stock Market speculation. Gold, diamonds, coffee, cocoa, sugar, jute, and cotton are sold over and over again before they've even been mined or harvested. Meanwhile, in the field, family farmers are deforesting parcels of land that will barely cover their own needs, and starving *mineiros* are clawing away at mountains, literally working themselves to the bone."

Disillusioned, he adds, "Take note: either Amazonia will be capitalist, or it will not."

[According to economist Piro Del Lasante,] "We've got to stop thinking in terms of short-term economic and political stakes. If we intend to make Amazonia our future, we must build it in a realistic fashion." But Prof. Oliveras Do Santos has his doubts. "Today the development of Amazonia is costing us as much as $10,000 for every settler who moves in. Only 5% of the country's population lives in a region that generates a scant 3% of the gross national product. Is all this really worth it?"

Manuella is twenty years old. A *mulata* from Rio's Beja Flore *favela*, among others. From her balcony—a piece of sheet metal propped up by two mostly untrimmed trees—she is taking a last, long look at the landscape before her. A sloping, squalid shantytown with 30,000 people crammed into every square kilometer, its only "urban parks" marijuana plants growing in gasoline cans. Her eyes tell you she is already somewhere else. Out there. She'll be leaving tomorrow. At dawn she'll load her hopes and yearnings onto a *pau-de-arara* (literally, "parrot's perch"), a wobbly, overheated public bus that will take a good week to cross Brazil. At journey's end, on the banks of some nameless river, she'll clear, then farm a small *fazeinde*, and her husband, Octavio, will work at the tin mine. Two more rainbow-chasers who'll make the Green Hell their home in hopes of getting their hands on its hidden wealth. The depths of myth are unfathomable.

Guy-Pierre Bennet
Dynasteurs, November 1987

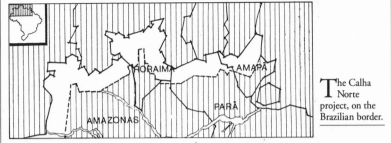

The Calha Norte project, on the Brazilian border.

The Elf-Aquitaine Affair

In the early 1980s, the government of Brazil granted the Braselfa Company, a subsidiary of Elf-Aquitaine, prospecting rights on Sateré-Mawé and Mundurucu territory in Amazonas state with the blessing of FUNAI, which seems to undermine the very spirit of its mission every chance it gets.

The prospectors cleared more than 185 miles of paths in the forest, placing dynamite charges as they went along; the explosions destroyed native crops and frightened away game. In addition, the Indians got hold of some charges that had been left behind, fuses and all, and, taking their cue from the workers they had been watching, tried to use them for fishing. The result was four fatal accidents. Workers' camps wreaked their usual havoc among the Indians by distributing liquor and inciting women to prostitution, all of which had a profoundly disturbing effect on Indian communal life.

Backed by the Brazilian Anthropological Association, the Indians protested to the authorities. Legal proceedings were instituted against Elf-Aquitaine, Braselfa, Petrobras (the state-run oil company), and FUNAI. An official communication was read before the Senate. Finally, the Brazilian Anthropological Association invited Simone Dreyfus-Gamelon, head of research at the Ecole des Hautes Etudes in France and an ethnologist specializing in Amazonia, to conduct an on-site investigation.

In 1984 a meeting took place in Manaus at the request of Simone Dreyfus. Seated across the table from one another were the representatives of the oil companies, the government agencies involved (including FUNAI), the Indian nations, and their allies and supporters (including the president of the Brazilian Association of Democratic Jurists).

Yielding to pressure, Braselfa closed up shop, and the Indians were awarded a fair settlement. They spent it on outboard motors so that they could market their own handicrafts at Manaus, where the local FUNAI agent, who had been acting as their go-between, was conscientiously stealing from them.

This affair, which the Brazilian press hailed as a "major first," will undoubtedly set a precedent. It adequately illustrates both the vulnerability of traditional native societies and the effectiveness of their self-help groups and the scientific institutions that support them.

Alain Gheerbrant

The Future

The threat with which the modern age has burdened the natives of Amazonia must be looked upon, not as a "regrettable" effect of development, but as an ongoing process that involves the integrity of our collective being. For the memory of the Indians is our memory, their heritage our heritage. The essence of humankind, like its history, is indivisible.

Indians: At the Frontier of Time

Darcy Ribeiro has never considered Indians research subjects; he has never put them under a microscope. He came to know and understand them by spending nearly ten years with them. He has won the right to mirror the way they think and, to some extent, speak on their behalf.

HENRI RAILLARD: When people talk about the Indian issue as if it were a problem that needs to be solved by whites, aren't they still expressing a colonialist attitude?

DARCY RIBEIRO: Indeed they are. We have to set something straight right from the start. It's wrong to talk about the "native issue" or the "Indian problem," because it's the other way around: The problem lies with society, with civilization. If the Indians hadn't endured centuries of invasions, they'd be doing very well at the present time.

H.R.: Did colonization cause ethnic groups to fragment from within?

D.R.: Yes, because everything is put in terms of tribes. When civilization came, it was like the plague: The Indians thought they were dealing with a tribe that was on equal footing with them, only to find out they were infinite in number. One day, an Indian who wanted to visit a city with me said, "It's frightening; they look like ants!" The arrival of the white man turned their values all topsy-turvy. They thought of themselves as a tribe that was beloved of their gods, and then suddenly along came this bigger, more powerful tribe.

Manaus shorefront.

This resulted in contention with their gods, with the tribal medicine man. They didn't know where they stood any more. The same with airplanes. As soon as they realized that their enemies were masters over these birds with rigid wings, they were completely baffled. With the coming of the white man, Indians were forced to ask themselves a host of serious questions about their very place in the changing scheme of things....

H.R.: Didn't the appearance of new diseases also have a more serious impact than people are generally willing to admit?

D.R.: A regular biological war broke out. That's why Cortés met no resistance when he landed in Mexico. Not only because he was considered a god, but because the soldiers quickly infected the entire populace. In no time, the city was littered with corpses, whereas a million soldiers could be mobilized at a moment's notice. Faced with this wave of disease, the medicine men found themselves completely at a loss and, as a result, called into question. So was Indian mythology itself. That was serious.

H.R.: Did the fact that Christians led these expeditions seem to have any importance?

D.R.: Of course it did! The attitude of the missionaries was a legacy of the crusades. We've got to put an end to this myth that Western civilization was truly Christian and charitable. On the contrary, it was the most brutal, most expansionist civilization ever known. And that goes for Protestant and Catholic alike....

H.R.: How would you describe the missionaries then?

D.R.: Missionaries were above all heretics. They took malicious pleasure in ridiculing everything that others held sacred, in defiling a tribe's most respected totems. A missionary's supreme joy was to be slain by an Indian, for his relationship was with God and only God, not with Indians. Indians were just a means to achieving saintliness.

H.R.: What brought on confrontations between Indians and whites?

D.R.: Whites have this feeling that they have a fundamental right to do what they do. They come with their view of what constitutes lawfulness and spell out Indian rights. Thus, they can allot land to the Indians and they can take it away, quite of their own accord. However, the land problem is not a major issue in Brazil because there are so few Indians. There used to be six million of them; now there are no more than 200,000.

There may have been a problem back when the number of Indians and outsiders was about the same, but that's no longer the case. Probably that's why, when open defiance does occur, be it in Brazil, Peru, or Bolivia, it is directed, not at the nation as a whole, but at the small-time, land-hungry peasants that live nearby. Brazil has a great many problems, but Indians are not one of them. At any rate, it is not a national problem....

H.R.: Well, then, what *do* they represent for Brazil?

D.R.: A challenge, nothing more. It's a matter of honor; the nation must not allow the remaining Indians to be killed.

That's why public opinion is the only weapon they've got. You can't pressure the nation into stopping the process. The defense, or offense, of the Indians in Brazil has gone through all these various phases.

The defense of the Indians did not get under way until 1910 with General Rondon, who was a positivist. There was a tremendous change. Whereas all the missionaries cared about was conversion, Rondon gave Indians the right to remain Indians, gave them land, let them live in peace. Lately, however, that's all changed considerably. FUNAI (the Brazilian government's Indian agency) has been placed in the hands of colonels who are extremely violent towards the Indians. For military dictatorship has established a highly authoritarian way of doing things throughout the country.

Also, there is another phenomenon that works against the Indians: immigration, mainly from Europe. Immigrants—General Geisel is a perfect example—wanted to turn Indians into "normal" people. That's because Geisel, who was president, fancied himself a dyed-in-the-wool Brazilian even though he was the son of Germans, spoke nothing but German until the age of twelve, and failed to understand that the Indians, who have been here for centuries, objected to being Brazilians like the rest.

It's because assimilation did not come about that Indian rights are scoffed at. This notion of assimilation came from the civilized world....

H.R.: And yet, interbreeding between the races does exist, doesn't it?

D.R.: Mulatto communities develop only insofar as Indian women are abducted and raped by white or blacks. The mixed population is negligeable at first, then it starts to grow. As it does, the indigenous population dwindles.

Occasionally, however, the Indians find themselves on the other side of the boundary with civilization. Only it's a shifting boundary, one that depends solely on civilization itself, which is why if the boundary gains ground, the Indians may find themselves cut off from their hunting or fishing grounds.

H.R.: But do you personally want Indians to have a role in society?

D.R.: Of course I do, but what I really want is for Indians to be represented in Brazilian political life. That approach comes from the Indians themselves, not me. The political arena has always been filled with people who know how to read and write; now it's time others were given a chance to speak.

H.R.: Ultimately, the relationship between Indians and civilization often boils down to problems of proportion...

D.R.: Of course, the problem can't be looked at the same way in all Latin American countries. On the one hand, there are sizable ethnic groups, like the Quechua (six million people) or the Aymara (ten million), that obviously carry some weight....

However, we must not forget that 90% of all Latin American Indians belong to small ethnic groups. Even so, there is reason to believe they are bound to be assimilated in the end. Naturally, they'll have to keep in touch with civilization (if only for medicine), but they won't be "civilized." There are some tribes which, although stripped of their land for over a century, have never been assimilated.

H.R.: What is the current attitude of the Church towards the Indians?

D.R.: There has been a major shift since Pope John XXIII. The Church in Latin America is in the process of rethinking

its history, of acknowledging mistakes that were made in the past, so much so that no one does a better job of protecting Indians nowadays than missionaries. For example, the Foucauld Friars who live among the Tapirapé have done an excellent job and have helped them rediscover some of their traditions. Thirty years ago there were a hundred Tapirapé; now there are more than five hundred. Still, some missions are out to undermine the Indians: the Salesians and the Protestants, for instance....

H.R.: Is there a difference between American and European anthropology?

D.R.: No, you can't say there are any real differences between the two, but all the same you've got to bear in mind that European anthropology has always been racist; its aim was to certify the superiority of the white man. It was part and parcel of colonialist policy, essentially inhuman, an anthropology of plunder. It did not take into consideration the conditions in which Indians lived; it was abstract and concerned solely with myths irrespective of their context, which was also a mistake from the scientific point of view. It was as if someone had studied the structure of the German family or the output of poetry in Berlin in 1945, during the bombings. It was utterly absurd.

At the present time, a new movement with a much fairer slant is gathering momentum, one that tends to give the

Indians their due and shows them what kind of people their ancestors were, in particular, by means of 19th-century photographs. This type of anthropology is far more scientific because it takes all factors into consideration. It is also far more responsible because it aims at producing books with the Indians, not at their expense.

H.R.: How can people in Brazil think of themselves as Indians or blacks?

D.R.: There will always be a tendency on the part of Brazilians to think of themselves as Indians or blacks; both are essential. Then there's the European side. In Brazil, it was good to feel European, very bad to be black, but not all that bad to feel like an Indian. That's why, for blacks, declaring they had some Indian blood in them was a way of living down their blackness. Thus, at one point in our history, there was a large, highly idealistic indigenous movement, mainly mulattos, that tried to forget their black roots by fabricating Indian ones....

H.R.: But didn't a pro-black movement come into being after that?

D.R.: Yes, there was a black movement in the 1960s, like the one in the United States. I saw its effects when I came back to Brazil after the coup d'etat. But there is also a tendency in Brazil for black movements to get sidetracked. People seem intent on confining them to things like the samba and other mundane aspects, to present a particular folkloric image of Brazilian blacks, to keep them from really searching for their roots.

When you see blacks in Rio wearing shirts with an American flag, or showing interest in Caribbean music or reggae, that's a genuine expression

of blackness, but lots of people find it upsetting.

H.R.: What forms are Indian defense movements taking today?

D.R.: We are witnessing the emergence of a new phenomenon. For young people, pro-Indian movements are no longer an expression of white guilt, but an acknowledgment that civilization has failed.... Brazil differs from the United States in that we are assimilationist: We accept blacks from the standpoint of a non-black Brazil, through interbreeding. The root ideology, the "whitening" of Brazil, is a racist ideology. But this ideology does not apply to Indians because there are too few of them. The Indians carry no weight in Brazil, which is why they may well disappear.

"Brazil"
Autrement, November 1982

Violence Escalates in Amazonia

A 1987 report on confrontations between gold miners, Indians, and believers in the Indian cause in a region that has proven rich in underground resources.

The upswing in violence in Amazonia has become especially acute today because mineral and rare-earth mining is expanding and most of all because a new Brazilian Constitution is being drawn up. It is the political event of the year, virtually eclipsing the problems of inflation and foreign debt. And the Indians, like all of the nation's minorities, want to make their voices heard in the drafting of this constitution, for the same reason the unions and professional guilds do.

An Amazonian construction site.

To be sure, the Indians themselves are voicing their demands, but they are not alone because a lobby of Indian defenders is growing on an international scale, rallying Catholic youth, missionaries, ethnologists, and ecologists to their cause. The latest action taken by this loosely defined support group was reported last week by the São Paulo daily *O Estadão,* which exposed an alleged international "conspiracy" to deprive Brazil of some of its sovereignty over Amazonia.

The principal defendants in this affair, which is beginning to sound like a detective novel, is CIMI—the Missionary Council for Indigenous Peoples—a Christian-based movement that is very active in defending Indian rights, and other groups farther afield, including, curiously enough, a tiny Catholic group based in Feldkirch (Liechtenstein). According to the São Paulo daily, CIMI wants the whole of Amazonia—from Venezuela, Colombia, and Peru to the Guyanas—to be recognized as part of a "world heritage" and set aside for the sole use of local indigenous peoples, and all clearing of land and mining operations banned.

CIMI has dismissed accusations that it is attacking [Brazil's] territorial integrity and continued to focus attention on its principal demands, which involve the protection of Indian land and rights. Under current Brazilian law, Indians are looked upon as semi-incompetents with no civil status or civil rights, but entitled thereby to permanent federal assistance, in particular, medical care. This assistance is administered by FUNAI, which, operating under adverse conditions, must see to the needs of an

I n the middle of the rain forest,
company housing.

estimated 220,000 people spread out
over numerous isolated or semi-
integrated tribes.

The conditions in which these
Indians live vary considerably
depending on their degree of
integration; but some of the most
isolated groups are getting special
attention because they have all too often
proven unstable when brought in
contact with civilization and because of
their importance as primitive tribes, as
part of a national heritage. Brazil's
Yanomami, which number between six
and nine thousand souls, comprise one
such group. And, as ill luck would have
it, one of the world's richest deposits of
gold and rare earths (uranium,
molybdenum, platinum, etc.) was
discovered on their land, along the
upper Río Negro.

Mineral prospecting and mining in
the area is being conducted by groups
like Mr. Lacombe's Paranapanema
Corporation, or Goldmazon, a concern
headed by Elton Röhnelt. In 1982, after
making a fortune in the timber
business, this colorful character decided
to devote himself, and his impressive
arsenal of logistical resources, to mineral
prospecting. He has since scoured

Amazonia and established a great many
prospecting centers; now he, too, is
taking charitable and missionary
organizations to task for their failure to
provide Indians with effective
assistance. On the subject of
"conspiracy," he denounces
international groups that are prepared
to do anything to prevent Brazilians
from tapping their own strategic
underground minerals.

For him, the inevitable solution to the
Indian problem must involve
integration—already partially achieved
except for isolated tribes that must be
spared—and sharing profits from
mining operations. As he sees it, this is
the only way to lift semi-integrated
Indians, living on land unfit for
agriculture, out of the stark poverty in
which they are now vegetating. But
Elton Röhnelt's good intentions
couldn't stop the uncontrollable influx
of *garimpeiros,* placer gold miners that
fear neither God nor man, who have
poured by the thousands into areas that
are officially off-limits.

Jean-Louis Peytavin
Le Figaro, 23 August 1987

Indian Power

A Continent Is Discovering its Individuality

With the rise in middle-class power,
Latin America began to accept the fact
that it is not purebred: Latin, yes, but
Indian, too. Latin American literature
thrust it into the world's collective face.
As a result, a new wave of researchers—
Latin American researchers—has begun
to appear, even in the forests. No more
living archaeology for them; instead, an
openness to the demands of peoples
they regard as fellow-countrymen and a

desire to help them make their voices heard. Thus, cracks in the vast wall of the Amazonian ghetto are starting to appear.

Various journals publish regular reports on the Amerindian situation, including updates on ongoing fieldwork. Concerned scientific and humanitarian organizations the world over, such as Cultural Survival (Boston), Survival International (London and Paris), and the Copenhagen-based International World Group for Indigenous Affairs (IWGIA) are another source of information.

A Privileged Interlocutor: The Missionary

A post-conciliar segment of the Church has followed suit and broken with the ethnocentrism of the past. Witness, in Brazil, the Missionary Council for Indigenous Peoples (CIMI), which has no qualms about crossing swords with FUNAI, if need be, or the Ecumenical Council for Indigenous Research (CEDIC), which is compiling with monkish patience an exhaustive list of native communities (four volumes published, eighteen in preparation).

In the field, we can take heart from the example set by the Salesians of the upper Orinoco, who, while respecting the identity of the Yanomami, are doing what they can to prepare them for their inevitable collision with civilization. Elsewhere, the Capucins and other missionaries are perpetuating the paternalism of yesteryear with limited success. The Summer Institutes of Linguistics and News Missions, natural allies of all Indian-killers, have incurred hatred wherever they go, and repeated scandals have prompted one country after

another to send them packing.

Cognizant of their trump cards, as well as of the dangers that need to be averted, the Indians have taken matters into their own hands in a number of places. Mutual aid societies have sprung up in Amazonia from villages right up to the national level.

At the top of this pyramid, which is in contact with the United Nations, is the Lima, Peru–based South American Indian Council (CISA), an associate member of the WCIP or World Council of Indigenous Peoples, of Bolivia. Other organizations include the Federation of Indigenous Nations of Ecuadorian Amazonia (ONIC), the Inter-Ethnic Association for the Development of the Peruvian Equatorial Forest (AIDESEP), the National Indigenous Organization of Colombia (ONIC), and the Union of Indian Nations of Brazil (UNI).

These Indians, who have proven that they are capable of sitting down at a negotiating table with whites, are struggling for their basic rights. They have successfully demonstrated that integration with the modern world need not inevitably lead to acculturation and impoverishment. But their success hinges on keeping the group from splintering. They know it. Of the 900,000 Indians living in Amazonia (1987), a good half are taking part in this operation. But what about the others? The Yanomami are an exemplary case in point. They illustrate the precarious condition of societies that are unwilling or unable to find a path that might lead them beyond the strictures of custom, beyond a world where time stands still, without destroying their bodies or souls.

Alain Gheerbrant

Chronology

1492 Christopher Columbus discovers America

1493 Pope Alexander VI issues the bull *Inter Caetera*, ceding to Portugal and Spain, respectively, all territory discovered to the east and west of a demarcation line 100 leagues west of the Azores

1494 Treaty of Tordesillas between Spain and Portugal shifts the demarcation line set by the *Inter Caetera* to 370 leagues west of the Azores, expanding Portugal's zone of exploration

1500 Amerigo Vespucci explores the Colombian and Venezuelan coasts and the mouths of the Amazon and the Orinoco; Portuguese explorer Pedro Alvares Cabral discovers Brazil; Vicente Yáñez Pinzón, Columbus' pilot, sights the mouth of the Amazon

1513 Vasco Núñez de Balboa of Spain crosses the Isthmus of Panama, becoming the first European to see the Pacific

1519–20 Magellan rounds the tip of South America during his circumnavigation of the globe

1519–26 Hernán Cortés conquers Mexico

1526 Sebastian Cabot sails up the Paraguay River

1532–5 Francisco Pizarro and Diego de Almagro conquer Peru

1537 Francisco de Orellana founds the city of Guayaquil

1538 Hernando Pizarro orders Diego de Almagro garotted

1541 The "Cinnamon Expedition" begins; mathematician and geographer Gerardus Mercator creates map distinguishing India from America

1542 24 August: Orellana reaches the mouth of the Amazon

1548 Gonzalo Pizarro beheaded

1560 Expedition of Pedro de Ursúa in search of the mythical El Dorado; mutiny led by Lope de Aguirre

1595 Expeditions of Sir Walter Raleigh and Laurence Keymis in Guiana

1617–8 Raleigh's second expedition to Guiana; Raleigh beheaded

1637–8 Captain Pedro de Teixeira leads expedition up the Amazon from Belém to Quito

1638–9 Teixeira and Father Acuña lead expedition from Quito to Belém, second downriver journey ever

1641 Cristobal de Acuña publishes *Nuevo Descubrimiento del Gran Río de las Amazonas* in Madrid

1669 Barra (now Manaus) founded

1743 Charles Marie de La Condamine sails down the Amazon

1760 Jesuits expelled from Brazil

1770 Joseph Priestley invents the rubber eraser

1799–1800 Alexander von Humboldt and Aimé Bonpland sail from the Orinoco to the Río Negro via the Casiquiare River

1817–20 German scientists Johann Baptist von Spix and Karl Friedrich Philipp von Martius sail up the Amazon and explore the Japurá and Madeira rivers

1822 Independence of Brazil

1823 Charles Macintosh invents rubber-coated waterproof material

1826–34 Alcide d'Orbigny ranges through South America

1839 Charles Goodyear invents vulcanization of rubber

1840–4 Robert Schomburgk explores the Guianas

1848 Alfred Russel Wallace and Henry Walter Bates leave for Amazonia

1850 Barra renamed Manaus and elevated to provincial capital

1888 John Boyd Dunlop invents the first pneumatic tire

1890 The Booth Line inaugurates transatlantic service between Liverpool and Manaus

1892 Edouard Michelin invents the detachable pneumatic tire

1896 Manaus Opera House opens

1910 Colonel Rondon founds Indian Protection Service

1912 Rubber plantations begin to flourish outside Amazonia; bankruptcies at Manaus

1948–50 Orinoco-Amazon Expedition: first crossing of the Sierra Parima (by Alain Gheerbrant, Pierre Gaisseau, Luis Saenz, and Jean Fichter)

1972 Indian Protection Service replaced by FUNAI

1975 Creation of the South American Indian Council

1988 3 June: New constitution of Brazil recognizes Indian rights to land and to profits from development of natural resources on that land

Further Reading

General

L'Art de la plume, exhibition catalogue. Muséum Nationale d'Histoire Naturelle, Paris, 1986

"Brésil," *Autrement,* vol. 44, Paris, November 1982

"Brésil," special issue of *Les Temps modernes,* No. 491, June 1987

Collier, Richard, *The River that God Forgot: The Story of the Amazon Rubber Boom,* Dutton, New York, 1968

Descola, Jean, *The Conquistadors,* trans. Malcolm Barnes, Viking Press, New York, 1957

Duviols, Jean-Paul, *L'Amérique espagnole vue et rêvée: les livres de voyages de Christophe Colomb a Bougainville,* Promodis, Paris, 1986

Englin, Jean, and Herve Théry, *Le Pillage de l'Amazonie,* Maspero, Paris, 1982

Frey, Peter, *Amazonie,* Payot, Paris, 1985

Freyre, Gilberto, *The Masters and the Slaves,* University of California Press, 1986

Handbook of South American Indians, Smithsonian Institution, Bureau of American Ethnology, Washington, D.C., 1950 (6 volumes)

Hemming, John, *Amazon Frontier: The Defeat of the Brazilian Indians,* Harvard University Press, Cambridge, 1987

———, *Red Gold: The Conquest of the Brazilian Indians,* Harvard University Press, Cambridge, 1978

Jaulin, Robert, *Le Livre blanc de l'ethnocide en Amérique,* Fayard, Paris, 1972

Lepargneur, François, *L'Avenir des Indiens au Brésil,* Le Cerf, 1975

Lévi-Strauss, Claude, *The Raw and the Cooked: Introduction to a Science of Mythology,* trans. John and Doreen Weightman, University of Chicago Press, 1983

———, *Tristes Tropiques,* trans. John and Doreen Weightman, Atheneum, New York, 1973

Mauro, Frédéric, *Histoire du Brésil,* "Que Sais-Je?," PUF, 1980

Métraux, Alfred, *Les Indiens d'Amérique du Sud,* ed. A.-M. Métailié, 1982

———, *Religions et magies Indiennes,* Gallimard, Paris, 1967

Niedergang, Marcel, *Les 20 Amériques Latines,* Le Seuil, Paris, 1962

Up de Graff, F. W., *Head-Hunters of the Amazon,* Herbert Jenkins Ltd., London, 1923

Von Hagen, Victor Wolfgang, *South America Called Them,* Knopf, 1945

Explorers' Accounts and Monographs

Acuña, Cristobal de, *Expedition into the Valley of the Amazons,* trans. Markham, 1859

Bates, Henry Walter, *The Naturalist on the River Amazons,* University of California Press, 1962

Bidou, Henry, *900 Lieues sur l'Amazone,* Gallimard, Paris, 1938

Biocca, Ettore, *Yanoáma,* trans. Dennis Rhodes, Dutton, New York, 1970

Carvajal, Gaspar de, *The Discovery of America,* trans. Bertram T. Lee, AMS Press, New York, 1970

Clastres, Pierre, *Chroniques des Indiens Guaranis,* Plon, 1972

Cousteau, Jacques-Yves and Mose Richards, *Jacques Cousteau's Amazon Journey,* Harry N. Abrams, Inc., New York, 1984

Creveaux, Jules, *Le Mendiant de l'Eldorado: de Cayenne aux Andes 1876–1879,* Phébus, 1987 (collected articles from the magazine *Le Tour du Monde*)

Gheerbrant, Alain, *Journey to the Far Amazon: An Expedition into Unknown Territory,* trans. Edward Fitzgerald, Simon and Schuster, New York, 1954

Humboldt, Alexander von, *Personal Narrative of Travels to the Equinoctial Regions of the New Continent during the Years 1799–1804,* AMS Press, New York, 1966

Huxley, Francis, *Affable Savages,* Viking Press, New York, 1957

Jaulin, Robert, *La Paix blanche,* 10–18, 1974

Kerjean, Alain, *Un Sauvage exil: Jacques Lizot, vingt ans parmi les Indiens yanomamis,* Seghers, Paris, 1988

La Condamine, Charles Marie de, *Voyage sur l'Amazone,* FM/La Découverte, Paris, 1981

Lizot, Jacques, *Tales of the Yanomami,* Cambridge University Press, New York, 1985

Pinkerton, John, *General Collection of the Best and Most Interesting Voyages and Travels in All Parts of the World,* volume 14, Longman, Hurst, Rees, Orme and Brown, London, 1813

Raleigh, Sir Walter, *The Discovery of the Empire of Guiana,* 1886

Reichel-Dolmatoff, Gerardo, *Amazonian Cosmos: The Sexual and Religious Symbolism of the Tukano Indians*, University of Chicago Press, 1971

Smith, Anthony, *Explorers of the Amazon*, Viking Press, New York, 1990

Amazonia in Literature

Amado, Jorge, *The Violent Land*, New York, 1965

Andrade, Mario de, *Macounaíma*, trans. E. A. Goodard, Random House, New York, 1984

Callado, Antônio, *Mon pays en croix*, Le Seuil, Paris, 1971

Carpentier, Alejo, *Le Partage des eaux*, Gallimard, Paris, 1955

Cendrars, Blaise, *Histoires vraies: en transatlantique dans la forêt vierge*, Grasset, Paris, 1936

Doyle, Sir Arthur Conan, *The Lost World*, Buccaneer Books, New York, 1977

Ferreira de Castro, José Maria, *Jungle: A Tale of the Amazon Rubber-Tappers*, trans. Charles Duff, Viking, New York, 1935

Gallegos, Rómulo, *Doña Bárbara*, Gallimard, Paris, 1931

Michaux, Henri, *Ecuador, Journal de voyage*, Gallimard, Paris, 1929

Ribeiro, Darcy, *Maíra*, Vintage Books, New York, 1984

Rivera, Jose Eustasio, *La Vorágine*, Biblioteca Ayachucho, 1985

Souza, Marcio, *The Emperor of the Amazon*, Avon Books, New York, 1980

———, *Mad Maria*, Avon, New York, 1985

Verne, Jules, *Eight Hundred Leagues on the Amazon*, Didier, New York, 1952

———, *Les Voyages extraordinaires*, Hetzel et Cie., 1898

List of Illustrations

Index

Acknowledgments

The publishers would like to thank the following individuals and organizations for their assistance in the production of this book: Jean-Bernard Gillot, bookseller; James Prunier, illustrator; and Ghislaine Taxy of the Interdoc Agency. Literary excerpts in Documentary section compiled by Ilda Dos Santos.

Photograph Credits

Aldus Book, London 13, 17a, 18a, 26a, 31, 44–5, 46, 46b, 47, 62b, 66a, 66b, 67a, 69, 79b. A.F.K., Münich 16, 62a, 64a, 76. Bibliothèque du Muséum, Paris 98a, 99b, 111a, 168, 169. Bibliothèque Nationale, Paris 38, 41, 42, 51, 68b, 97, 131. Bridgeman Library, London 12, 100–1, 102–3, 104–5. Nino Cirani 36. Charmet, Paris 48, 96, 100–1, 102–3, 104–5, 148. Giancarlo Costa, Rome 21, 22a, 166r. Dagli-Orti, Paris 11, 14, 15a, 18b, 22b, 39, 57, 63, 108a, 112–3. Dominique Darbois 141. E.T. Archives, London 67b. Explorer Archives, Paris 27, 58. Gamma/Adams, Paris 126a. Gamma/Collart-Odinetz, Paris 35, 119. Gamma/Dutilleux, Paris 120b, 122. Gamma/Morel, Paris 124, 176. Yann Garcia 114, 137, 143. Alain Gheerbrant 129, 134, 138, 144. Giraudon, Paris 15b, 17b, 29, 40a, 40b, 54–5, 56, 60l, 60r, 61l, 130. Hoa-Qui/Marc Bruwier, Paris 120a, 127. I.G.D.A. Archives, Milan 43, 44a. The Illustrated London News, London 94–5. Magnum/Bruno Barbey, Paris 32–3, 34. Agence Marco Polo, Paris 37, 125. Mas, Barcelona 24–5. Kimball Morrisson, London 88–9, 92a, 156, 163, 179, 180, 182. Musée de l'Homme, Paris 108b, 123. Peter Newark's, London 59r. Private collection Cover, 1–11, 26b, 28a, 28b, 50b, 52–3, 68a, 70–1, 72, 73, 74, 75, 77r, 79a, 82, 83, 84–5, 87, 89b, 90–1, 92b, 93, 106, 107a, 107b, 110, 158, 161. Rights Reserved 121, 126b, 166, 170, 171. Roger-Viollet, Paris 19, 78, 132–3, 142. Scala, Florence 30. Service Historique de la Marine, Vincennes 50. Société de Géographie, Paris 86a, 86b. Staats-bibliothek, Munich 152. Studio Pizzi, Rome 118. Tallandier, Paris 164. Tapabor, Paris 49, 61r, 80, 81a, 81b.

Text Credits

Grateful acknowledgment is made for use of material from the following works: Andrade, Mario de, *Macounaíma*, trans. E. A. Goodard, 1984. Reprinted by permission of Random House, Inc. ("Amazonia, Birthplace of Macounaíma"). Bates, Henry Walter, *Naturalist on the River Amazons*, foreword by Robert L. Usinger. Copyright © 1962 The Regents of the University of California ("The Gaze of the Scientist"). Biocca, Ettore, *Yanóama*, trans. Dennis Rhodes, 1971. Reprinted by permission of the publisher, Dutton, an imprint of New American Library, a division of Penguin Books, USA, Inc. ("Chimila Shamans"). Carvajal, Gaspar de, *The Discovery of America*, trans. Bertram T. Lee, AMS Press, New York, 1970 ("The Río de Orellana"). Castro, Ferreira de, *Jungle: A Tale of the Amazon Rubber-Tappers*, trans. Charles Duff, 1935. Reprinted by permission of Viking Penguin, a division of Penguin Books, USA, Inc. ("The Force of the Jungle"). Gheerbrant, Alain, *Journey to the Far Amazon: An Expedition into Unknown Territory*, trans. Edward Fitzgerald, Victor Gollancz Ltd., London; Simon and Schuster, New York, 1954 ("First Encounter with the Guaharibo," "The Sierra Parima"). Levi-Strauss, Claude, *The Raw and the Cooked: Introduction to a Science of Mythology*, trans. John and Doreen Weightman, vol. 1, 1983. Copyright © 1969 by Harper & Row, Publishers Inc. Reprinted by permission of HarperCollins Publishers. ("How Birds Acquired Their Colored Plumage"). Up de Graff, F. W., *Head-Hunters of the Amazon*, Herbert Jenkins Ltd., 1923 ("The Anaconda")

Born in Paris in 1920, Alain Gheerbrant is a poet, writer, filmmaker, and explorer. After a brief stint as an avant-garde publisher, he left for Bogotá, where he organized and led the Orinoco-Amazon Expedition (1948–50). He was the first to cross the Sierra Parima and make peaceful contact with the Yanomami (or Guaharibo, as they were then known). He then traveled the world, conducting research and writing articles that led to a number of books and films.

Translated from the French by I. Mark Paris

Project Manager: Sharon AvRutick
Typographic Designer: Elissa Ichiyasu
Design Assistant: Tricia McGillis
Text Permissions: Ellen Wallenstein
Editorial Interns: Sibyl Ehresmann, Jennifer Stockman

Library of Congress Catalog Card Number: 91–75502

ISBN 0–8109–2860–4

Copyright © Gallimard 1988

English translation copyright © 1992 Harry N. Abrams, Inc.,
New York, and Thames and Hudson Ltd., London

Published in 1992 by Harry N. Abrams, Incorporated, New York
A Times Mirror Company

Printed and bound in Italy by Editoriale Libraria, Trieste